GUIDE TO SUCCESSFUL CHRISTIAN TEACHING

by

Ardell Jacquot

American Association of Christian Schools
P.O. Box 1097, Independence, MO 64051

TABLE OF CONTENTS

FOREWORD

In order for teaching to take place, you must have a teacher and a reasonably cooperative student. In order for one to become a success-ful teacher, there are certain traits that must be incorporated into the life of a good teacher. Discipline, authority, a quest for excellence, en-thusiasm, and a godly wisdom to establish the right priorities within a given classroom are just a few of those qualities.

Dr. Ardell Jacquot is a master of the education profession. He is able to command the attention of college students, junior high school students, or a convention of his peers. He exhibits those qualities that a good teacher must have, and he is able to effectively convey in an in-formative and entertaining manner the various techniques that a good teacher might use in his or her classroom. This book, **Guide to Success-ful Christian Teaching** should be beneficial in establishing a practical philosophy for new teachers; for communicating helpful procedures for experienced teachers; and for giving uplifting inspiration to tired teachers.

Christian education has been greatly blessed by the consecrated abilities of men and women such as Dr. Jacquot. Teachers who want to excel in their teaching will want to glean from this **Guide to Successful Christian Teaching**.

Dr. Jacquot is an outstanding Christian, and he is a great family person. All of his children have attended Christian schools. He and his wife Dorothy are both graduates of Christian institutions. I have observed him as a teacher, church member, and friend. I know that this book is a must for every Christian school teacher.

Dr. Al Janney
President (1972-1992)
American Association of Christian Schools

Teaching
As A
Ministry

Chapter 1

I
TEACHING AS A MINISTRY

At a Christian teachers' convention the speaker asked how many ministers were in the assembly. Although the auditorium was packed with hundreds of Christian teachers and administrators, only about twelve pastors raised their hands. The speaker then read a definition of the word "minister" to the group. A minister, he said, was one who acts under orders or authority of another; or . . . attends to the wants and comforts of someone. "To minister is also to give aid; to serve; to do things needful or helpful."[1]

Most people think that only pastors of churches are ministers, and certainly they are; but in a broad sense all servants of God are His ministers. In II Corinthians 3:5-6 Paul declares to all the Corinthians, "Not that we are sufficient of ourselves to think any thing as of ourselves; but our sufficiency is of God; Who also hath made us able *ministers* of the new testament . . ." Again in the same book, the apostle, through the inspiration of the Holy Spirit, continues to stress the ministry of the Christian worker:

> We then, as workers together with Him, beseech you also that ye
> receive not the grace of God in vain. Giving no offence in any thing,
> that the ministry be not blamed: But in all things approving ourselves
> as the ministers of God . . . (II Corinthians 6:1, 3, 4a).

Hopefully every Christian teacher will see himself as the Lord's servant, who ministers as one sent " . . . to give aid; to serve; to do things needful or helpful . . ." to meet the spiritual, mental, and physical needs

4

of young people in school. The teaching ministry is that of helping boys and girls to know about God and to learn how to live their lives in the light of the Bible.

Ephesians 4:11-12 states:

> And He gave some apostles; and some, prophets; and some, evangelists; and some, pastors and teachers; for the perfecting of the saints, for the work of the ministry, for the edifying of the body of Christ.

Teachers find themselves mentioned in the above verses along with evangelists and pastors; they are considered full-time servants of God. The above verses also indicate that teachers have the responsibility to help young people develop spiritually, to labor in the service of the Lord, and to instruct others through their lives and words. As Byrne says, "Teaching is important because it is a sacred ministry."[2]

REQUISITES IN THE MINISTERING TEACHER'S LIFE

The teaching ministry can be accomplished only by the power of the Holy Spirit, "not by might, nor by power, but by My Spirit, saith the Lord of Hosts" (Zechariah 4:6). When a Christian worker attempts to influence young people, he should not rely on his own personality or intellect, but on the work of the Holy Spirit. In order for the Spirit of God to use the servant-teacher effectively, there are definite requirements that must be met.

Die to Self

One must die to self as stated in the Scriptures: "I am crucified with Christ: nevertheless I live; yet not I, but Christ liveth in me and the life which I now live in the flesh I live by the faith of the Son of God, Who loved me, and gave Himself for me." (Galatians 2:20). When the ministering teacher dies to self, the life of self-denial comes into play. Howse thinks of this self-denial as "the God-man relationship — God working through persons to accomplish His work in the world."[3]

Surrender to God

The Christian teacher must make an unconditional surrender of everything. Such surrender will include an individual's body, mind, time, ambitions, talents, possessions, family, and anything else that could usurp the Lord's rightful preeminence in his life.

Love for Others

In addition to self-denial and unconditional surrender, a Christian worker must have love for others. Dr. Bob Jones, Jr. states the requirement this way: "The Christian is not under the Old Testament Law, but we are slaves and captives of grace which carries with it the obligation to be bound by a higher law — the law of love."[4] This law of love is demonstrated in at least two ways:

Love for Students. This is not a love of emotion; it is not being drawn to the physically attractive, but rather "It involves a recognition of the peculiar needs of that one whom Jesus loves, and whom He asks us to care for for His sake,"[5] says Trumbull. The Christian worker's methods will only be effective to the degree he loves his pupils and to the degree he comes to know their problems and interests.

An Inner Desire to Share. God has given to every true teacher a fundamental desire to share his knowledge with others. Whether that knowledge is spiritual or intellectual, when the Spirit of God empowers him, the Christian teacher's instruction will be sprinkled with grace and truth. The satisfaction of knowing that he has helped his students understand something that has previously been unfamiliar is the reward of the sharing teacher.[6]

QUALIFICATIONS OF THE MINISTERING TEACHER

Natural Qualifications

Whoever would undertake the training of young people should also possess at least some of the following qualities and abilities:

Ability to Teach. There are some who have tremendous mental abilities, yet they are unable to explain their ideas clearly to others. Still others are able to expound facts in an understandable fashion, but their lives have little or no effect on their pupils. The influential Christian is the person who imparts "knowledge which possesses power to impress the heart, move the will, and prompt action."[7]

Sincerity. Sincerity should be at the top of anyone's list of desirable personality traits for the individual who desires to be influential with others. Insincerity is easily detected by the pupils, and they soon lose confidence in the actions and words of the insincere teacher. Because the teacher wants the confidence of his students, his prayer should be, "Lord, keep me sincere."

Enthusiasm. The aim of every great teacher is to set his pupils on fire so that they in turn will go from the classroom to live an ardent Christian life. When a Christian worker is enthusiastic in his teaching, that enthusiasm will be infectious.[8]

Patience and Perseverance. Helping young people become what they should be for the Lord is a slow and drawn out process; therefore, the Christian leader should not get discouraged when he runs into difficulties or when he does not immediately encounter success. Wilkes says,

> Patience and perseverance must be learned by practice, and, indeed, they can be learned if one honestly tries and persists in trying.

The Christian teacher will remember the patience of God, Who never tires in leading us in the straight path though we lapse ever so often. And since Paul admonished us to be patient toward all men (I Thessalonians 5:14), we should certainly be patient toward our pupils.[9]

Common Sense. Many situations arise in the training of children that call for the use of tact and common sense. The teacher's common sense must tell him what to do and what effect his procedures will have on others. Knowing what to do and what to say at the right time is common sense.

Self-Control. "Keep cool," Koehler declares, "and do not let any personal resentment or blinding passion obscure your vision to the noble aim of your work."[10] Praying for God's help to control one's temper and preserve one's evenness of mind is essential for success. Certainly one of the greatest victories is to control and to conquer one's self.

Spiritual Qualifications

In a spiritual sense the teacher is the shepherd of his class because the Lord has given him the responsibility to minister to the eternal needs of those entrusted to his care; therefore, he should have the following spiritual qualifications:

Love for Christ. The Lord continues to ask, "Lovest thou Me?" Proper love for Christ will cause the teacher to have the correct attitude and will move him to be faithful no matter what the circumstances. Again, Koehler says, "A work of love is never grievous and burdensome; and feeding the lambs of Christ is, and should be, a work of love."[11]

Faith. There is no attribute that surpasses faith, for by it the heroes of the Bible conquered the impossible; and, in like manner, the child of God that stands before his students will trust in God to do for him what he cannot do for himself.

Consecration. The Lord Jesus Christ must have the preeminence in the life of the teacher, and this can only be accomplished with an unconditional surrender to Christ. William Borden prayed, "Lord Jesus, I take hands off as far as my life is concerned. I put Thee on the throne in my heart. Change, cleanse, use me as Thou shalt choose."[12]

Prayer. Prayerlessness is a sin because the Lord Himself told His children that they should always pray; consequently, the Christian teacher should daily talk to God concerning himself and his pupils. "Let intercession be a real longing for the souls of those around us," said Andrew Murray, "a real bearing of the burden of their sin and need, a real pleading for the extension of God's kingdom."[13]

Knowledge of the Scriptures. In order to impart clear biblical knowledge, the ministering teacher must have a thorough knowledge of Scriptural doctrines. He should never be content with what he knows, but he must continually study for more perfect knowledge. Any teacher who does not have the Bible at the center of his life and thought or who does not live daily in the Book cannot hope to develop as he should for the Lord, nor will his influence be felt as God would have it.[14]

Byrne declares, "Christian teaching, therefore, is a ministry; it is an art which demands time and careful preparation. It demands the best that we can give it."[15] An individual will succeed if he is willing to pay the price in spiritual preparation and in developing a godly personality.

THE TEACHING MINISTRY IS . . .

Meeting Students' Needs

"It is the need of the pupil that we are trying to meet,"[16] comments Rozell. Thus, in the process of directing the students into various learning experiences, the teacher's communication must always be on the level of the pupils or else it will be wasted.

Relating Knowledge to Life

Rozell further believes that the presentation of ideas, facts, or opinions must lead logically and emotionally to the applications that the teacher had in mind for the student.[17] Aiding the teacher in making ideas relevant to young people is the Bible, which deals not merely with abstract truth, but with real life.[18]

Developing . . .

Attitudes. Campbell says, "An attitude is like a key; a wrong attitude closes a door, and a right attitude opens it."[19] Attitudes indicate how an individual will behave in different situations; therefore, the ministering teacher must instill godly attitudes in the life of each student.

Loyalties. Loyalties are closely related to attitudes. Loyalty is an individual's devotion to a person, a cause, or a truth. Again Campbell declares, "It involves fidelity, allegiance and love; it suggests action and secures steadfastness of purpose."[20] Sometimes when loyalty is misplaced, a student is loyal to the wrong kind of person or to an unworthy cause, but the responsibility of the Christian worker is to guide and direct those in his charge to measure their loyalties against the Word of God.

Abilities. Skills in the mental, physical, and spiritual realm are called abilities, and because they are learned, they can be improved. When these abilities are steered in the right direction, they will develop into useful habits which in turn become automatic in practice; therefore, "Abilities, habits, and skills are vital among the objectives for ministering teachers."[21]

Contentment. Christian contentment does not consist in the ease of life. Fuller believes that contentment enables an individual to realize that, though a Christian has little of this world's goods, that little is sufficient when God is in it.[22] If young people see that their teachers are happy and content with their serviçe for God, then students will know that "godliness with contentment is great gain" (I Timothy 6:6).

Purity. Chalmers says that purity is being clean and free from sin's control. Purity settled in the heart by the Holy Spirit will bring moral victories.[23] Because the modern world laughs at purity, students today have a greater need than ever for their teachers to be examples of purity.

Courage. Courage is doing right in spite of what other people think or say; it sometimes means standing alone. However, the Christian can be assured that God's promise will be his: "Be strong and of a good courage, fear not nor be afraid of them; for the Lord thy God, He it is that doth go with thee; He will not fail thee, nor forsake thee" (Deuteronomy 31:6).

Goals. Goals give direction and meaning to a student's life. Thus, the teacher should help the student to define worthwhile goals for his life, goals that are made in the light of God's Word.[24]

HOW A TEACHER MINISTERS TO STUDENTS

Teaching has always been of utmost importance in God's plan because Scriptural truth delivered by the power of the Holy Spirit will result in changed lives for Christ. Consequently, the Christian teacher who wants to minister to students should keep the following things in mind.

Educating the Heart

It has been said that the heart of education is the education of the heart.[25] There can be no true Christian education if the outward only is changed yet the inward is not. "Keep thy heart with all diligence," Solomon said, "for out of it are the issues of life" (Proverbs 4:23).

Teaching by Doctrine

By having their minds and hearts filled with the doctrines of the Bible, the students will experience growth from within and will have a resource of Scriptural truths on which to draw for their lives. When a Christian teacher incorporates strong, doctrinal principles in his teaching, he not only refutes error and heresy, but also defends the students against the inroads of the flesh, the world, and the devil. Through the education of Bible doctrines, he protects the souls of boys and girls and strengthens them in the faith of Christ.[26]

Having Proper Expectations

Betts states,

> The child comes into school with much potential and very little actual capital. The powers of the mind and soul at first lie dormant,

waiting for the awakening that comes through the touch of the world about and for the enlightenment that comes through instruction.[27]

Every teacher should set his standards high, but not demand the impossible. Children are children in knowledge, in understanding, in experience, and in character; and because of their immaturity, the teacher should not expect them to already know what he is going to teach them nor to already be what he intends to make of them with the help of God.[28]

Knowing the Material to Be Taught

In order to minister as he should, the instructor must know the accomplishments the students should achieve during the lesson period. When he has prepared his lesson sufficiently, he will be able to stand before the class with a full mind and a clear understanding of the material. Such preparation demands adequate research into additional subject matter and plans for the use of appropriate visual aids.

Showing Enthusiasm

Because young people respond to extra energy expended by the instructor, enthusiasm is something worth striving for. When the teacher is excited about his subject, youngsters will be stimulated to think and to participate, and their time in class will be more interesting and profitable.[29]

CONCLUSION

In the words of H.W. Byrne, "Christian teaching is a ministry; it is an art which demands time and careful preparation."[30] By offering himself to Christ every day, the Christian teacher provides himself as the vessel; he already has the message which is the Word of God. Like Christ he must see his students as sheep without a shepherd and be moved by a tender heart toward them. That kind of motivation will make the servant of God the fruitful minister that the Lord would have him to be.[31]

A.A. Baker sums it up this way:

> An evangelistic emphasis and a spiritual ministry with boys and girls — what a thrill it is to know that we can have a part in a ministry that will pay dividends throughout this lifetime and throughout eternity, a living investment in the lives of boys and girls. The Lord Himself tells us to 'suffer the little children and forbid them not, to come unto me: for of such is the kingdom of heaven.' (Matthew 19:14)[32]

FOOTNOTES

[1]*Webster's Third New International Dictionary* (Unabridged) 1963 G.&C. Merriam Company, Pub., Springfield, Mass.

[2]H.W. Byrne, *Christian Education for the Local Church* (Grand Rapids, Michigan: Zondervan Publishing House, 1973), p. 247.

[3]W.L. Howse, *Those Treasured Hours* (Nashville, Tennessee: Broadman Press, 1960), p. 59.

[4]Bob Jones, Jr., "Editorial," *Faith for the Family,* February 1981, p. 2.

[5]H. Clay Trumbull, *Teaching and Teachers* (New York: Charles Scribner's Sons, 1906), p. 285.

[6]Doak S. Campbell, *When Do Teachers Teach* (Nashville, Tennessee: Broadman Press, 1935), p. 95.

[7]Edward A. Koehler, *A Christian Pedagogy* (New Ulm, Minnesota: Martin Albrecht, Publisher, n.d.), p. 42.

[8]L. Wilkes, *Teach Yourself to Teach* (London: English Universities Press Ltd., 1952), p. 9.

[9]Koehler, pp. 55-56.

[10]Ibid., pp. 77-78.

[11]Ibid., p. 55.

[12]A.B. Simpson, *Standing on Faith* (London: Marshall, Morgan and Scott Ltd., 1934), pp. 1-2.

[13]Andrew Murray, *The School of Obedience* (London: Marshall, Morgan and Scott Ltd., n.d.), p. 64.

[14]Frank E. Gaebelein, *The Pattern of God's Truth* (Chicago: Moody Press, 1968), p. 45.

[15]Byrne, p. 248.

[16]Ray Rozell, *Talks on Sunday School Teaching* (Grand Rapids, Michigan: Zondervan Publishing House, 1969), pp. 32-33.

[17]Ibid, pp. 94-95.

[18]J. Edward Hakes, *An Introduction to Evangelical Christian Education* (Chicago: Moody Press, 1964), p. 45.

[19]Campbell, p. 29.

[20]Ibid., p. 30.

[21]Ibid., p. 31.

[22]Andrew Fuller cited in *Gems from Christian Writers* (London: W. Clowes and Sons, n.d.), pp. 96-97.

[23]Thomas Chalmers cited in *Gems from Christian Writers* (London: W. Clowes and Sons, n.d.), pp. 96-97

[24]Campbell, p. 15.

[25]Koehler, p. 103.

[26]Ibid., p. 144.

[27]G.H. Betts, *The Teaching of Religion* quoted in *A Christian Pedagogy* (New Ulm, Minnesota: Martin Albrecht Publisher, n.d.), p. 77.

[28]Koehler, p. 77.

[29]Guy P. Leavitt, *Teach With Success* (Cincinnatti, Ohio: Standard Publishing, 1956), p. 55.

[30]Byrne, p. 248.

[31]Ibid., p. 249.

[32]A.A. Baker, *The Successful Christian School* (Pensacola, Florida: A Beka Book Publication, 1979), p. 29.

QUESTIONS AND PROBLEMS

1. Why do you think there are some teachers who do not realize that teaching in a Christian school is a ministry as sacred as that of being a preacher or a missionary?

2. How might a pastor help the teachers in his Christian school be aware of their ministry to others?

3. Under "Spiritual Qualifications" in this chapter, which of the subheadings do you consider to be the most important? Give reasons for your answer.

4. Would increasing the salaries of Christian school teachers make their ministries more effective? Would higher salaries draw better teachers to Christian schools? Would you like to see teachers in Christian schools make as much as those in public schools? Why?

5. What do you consider to be the main reason teachers are not more effective in the ministry of teaching?

6. Can the ministry of teachers be gauged by the type of young people who graduate from their schools? For instance, what percent are called into fulltime Christian work, attend Christian colleges, or desire to return to the school and teach?

7. Are you aware of times when the Spirit of God is working through you as a teacher? Are you always aware of God's Spirit working?

8. Can you think of any other natural or spiritual qualification needed by the teacher that is not mentioned by the author?

Relationships
Of The
Teacher

Chapter 2

II
RELATIONSHIPS OF THE TEACHER

The relationships of any man or woman are numberless and vary according to the individual. In fact, to trace a person's relationships to parents, pastors, teachers, and other friends would be to produce the history of a lifetime.

Teachers have varied relationships that are broad in scope, for they deal with principals, pastors, parents, students, and other teachers. Not only does the teacher have contact with many different types of people, but he must also have a distinct relationship with God and His Holy Word because from the Word of God the Christian worker receives precepts by which he can pattern his life. The degree to which his relationships are handled will determine to a great extent the success or failure of the teacher.

RELATIONSHIP TO GOD

The first and most important commitment for the Christian teacher is his relationship to God. To have such a relation, the teacher must first be a Christian; in other words, he must be born again. As Percy Parker says,

> The Christian life is a glorious life. Those who try to live the Christian life before they have reached it do not find it glorious, but those who have 'got it' find it a life full of unspeakable joy and glory.[1]

God must be made the ruler of the teacher's life, and when He is, the child of God will be obedient to his Father. "True obedience," as Murray expresses that relationship, "is born of love and inspired by it . . . it also opens the way unto the love of God."[2] Proper love will produce the correct attitude of respect towards God which in turn will develop a belief that God is the one true sovereign Lord of all.

The teacher should also regard God as the supreme Provider, for He will take care of the teacher in any situation just as a shepherd does his sheep.[3]

Prayer is also essential for a healthy relationship in the Christian's fellowship with the Lord. If all the Scriptural conditions for prayer are met, it will be a powerful tool in the teacher's life. A teacher can attain success because answers to prayer extend to all of the promises of God.[4] The prayer life of the teacher is part of the dedication of his efforts to God.

The Christian instructor can certainly profit by following the example of the Master Teacher, the Lord Jesus Christ. Eavey says that the words, "He taught in their synagogues," and similar expressions occur over and over again in the Gospels.[5] Those that heard Christ preach the Sermon on the Mount marveled, ". . . for He taught them as One having authority."[6]

The influence of the believer is meaningless unless the living Spirit of God acts upon his heart, life, and lips. Especially is this true of the teacher, for "the spirit of the learner must meet with the spirit of the teacher, and the Holy Spirit must impart eternal truth to the one through the other as a medium."[7] Eavey writes,

> First, last, and always, the truly Christian teacher will realize his utter dependence upon the Spirit of God. The work that he is doing is God's work; he himself can never be other than a channel through which God operates. So the Christian teacher can put his trust in the Holy Spirit to guide and to work through him, making him more and more nearly perfect in teaching God's truth to man.[8]

RELATIONSHIP TO THE BIBLE

The Word of God represents the foundational source of faith and the means through which the Holy Spirit brings conviction to the heart of the teacher. As a result, the Bible is his only textbook on living because through the Scriptures he is able to find God's will. However, he must approach the Scriptures in complete faith if he is to "love it, and yield to it, and keep it."[9] Eavey says,

> The Christian teacher realizes how imperative it is that his aim be closely allied to the study and use of the Bible. In the Scriptures are to be found the only aims that can stand the test; from the Bible it is

possible to construct for every man and every group of men a series of aims sufficient for every demand of life, individual and social. 'The way of man is not in himself.' What man devises is not sufficient for direction of self or of others. Only the truth revealed in the Bible has power to transform life and build character. The aim of the Christian teacher is found in the Bible, the revelation of God to man concerning his state, his need, his salvation, and his destiny.[10]

Because the Bible has these qualifications, the Christian instructor should read it daily. Such reading will result in a desire for wisdom (James 1:5); a surrendered body (Romans 12:1-2); a trust for fruition (John 15:16); a request for power, love, and a sound mind (II Timothy 1:7); a trust in the Lord (Proverbs 3:5-7); and death to self (John 12:24). Certainly, there are many other results to be gained by faithfully reading the Word of God.

RELATIONSHIP TO PRAYER

Along with the reading of God's Word is the privilege of prayer. Murray believed that prayer can be a time of strengthening for the Christian teacher:

> How unspeakably gracious, that in the morning hour the bond that unites us with God can be so firmly tied, and during hours when we have to move amid the rush of men and duties, and can scarce think of God, the soul can be kept safe and pure . . .[11]

Prayer should include a time of confession in which the Christian can rid himself of any barriers between him and God. The prayer of confession should be followed by a petition for grace.[12] At the same time, there should be a request for a love for God and other people as commanded in Matthew 22:37, 39. Thus, the teacher's prayer life should be seasoned with requests, confession, and grace if he is to know the victorious life that Christ desires him to live.

RELATIONSHIP TO THE LOCAL CHURCH

The church was founded by Jesus Christ; it is the only institution for which Christ gave His life. If He placed such importance upon it, teachers should also give allegiance and attention to it, for believers need the preaching and fellowship found in the local assembly. The preaching of the Word of God contains the admonition necessary to keep sin out of the Christian's life, whereas Christian fellowship is the encouragement from others to do God's will — and certainly everyone needs to be admonished and encouraged to stay on the right track.[13]

Attendance and support of a Scriptural church identify the teacher as an active Christian. Genuine service in the local church reveals an individual to be a committed servant of God. The church influences a Christian in every area of life, all the way from fellowship and Christian living to spiritual growth and soul winning. Above all else, the church is a place of worship, which gives a sense of oneness with God, brings awareness of limitations, produces strength, and renews a desire for service.[14]

RELATIONSHIP TO THE PRINCIPAL

Developing the proper attitude for those in authority is absolutely essential in the life of the teacher. This relationship to authority is of vital importance, for as the teacher learns submission to the principal of the school, his class will learn submission to him. The purpose of authority is to provide three things: growth in wisdom and character, protection from temptations, and direction for decisions.[15]

One truth that the Christian worker should realize is that he must follow and be loyal to people who may very well be inferior to him in experience, spirituality, or knowledge; but no matter what defect the leader has, a teacher is under that authority, and he must obey and be a follower.[16] Deuteronomy 11:27 sets before the teacher a curse for disobedience and a blessing for obedience; therefore, obedience is the key to a proper relationship with the administration.[17]

The teacher's day-to-day relationship with the administrator must be based upon Biblical guidelines. In accordance with these, the teacher is to be silent rather than make any detrimental comment about the principal (Titus 3:1-2). Since God has ordained "higher powers" to direct and to lead, the Christian worker should not resist the powers that have been placed over him (Romans 13:1-2), but should be submissive to the regulations and directions of those over him. Only then will the servant of God receive "the praise of them that do well."[18]

Due to the nature of his position, the principal will have to deliver suggestions and judgments to the teacher from time to time. It is hoped that these matters will be seasoned with praise in the worker's area of strength. However, the only way an individual can improve in his effectiveness is to learn his weaknesses and work on them. Even if the administrator might seem to be unduly critical, the Christian teacher should remember that the Lord is trying to purify him for His service.[19]

There have been too few who have taken criticism properly as being from God; and as a result, many have missed the refining craftsmanship of the Holy Spirit. The devil tempts the servant of God through discouragement and through self-pity, which will bring defeat. Therefore, the Christian teacher should learn to take criticism; for if it is not spiritually digested, criticism will lead to spiritual heartburn.

Circumventing the principal's authority is not uncommon in certain Christian schools, especially when the employee happens to be close to the pastor, a deacon, or a board member. The effectiveness of the whole school program is hindered when a teacher bypasses the principal and seeks assistance from someone higher in the order-of-command. A pastor may be flattered that his power is sought, but little does he realize the devastating effect such a response has on the morale of the principal and other teachers.

RELATIONSHIP TO SUPERVISORS

The next position of authority that a teacher might have to relate to is that of a supervisor. Not all of the Christian schools are large enough to have these special teachers to assist the administration; however, if a school does have supervisors, it is the responsibility of each teacher to submit to their suggestions and instructions. Whether on a grade level or departmental level, the instructor will be working more with the supervisor than with anyone else; therefore, proper respect is due that individual because of his ability and experience.

The supervisor should be a friend and a help to those teachers under his charge. He should aid others in such areas as school policies, room appearance, scheduling, location of materials, teaching techniques, implementation of new ideas, and curriculum development.

RELATIONSHIP TO OTHER TEACHERS

Every responsible adult usually finds himself working with others in some way or another, and of course, the teacher's work is no exception. His relationship with his fellow teachers will play a vital role in his happiness and success; consequently, he must have a proper attitude toward those with whom he labors. His good works will simply be a demonstration of the reality of his faith.

Everyone appreciates an individual whose uncomplaining spirit and encouraging words make the school year a pleasurable experience. Not only will the school benefit by having such people around, but each teacher can reap the enjoyment of lifelong friendships when he himself works at becoming such a person. Redpath calls attention to the relationship shared by two well-known, ancient colleagues, Paul and Epaphroditus,

> Paul describes him [Epaphroditus] as 'my brother, my fellow worker . . .' Paul had discovered these qualities in this man's life as they lived together in prison. 'My brother.' They shared the same parenthood. They were born of God . . . What times they must have had together! Perhaps whole nights were spent with one another recording and telling each other things that God had done for them . . . Both of these men just lived at the cross, and out from there flowed the sympathy and love of the Lord Jesus . . . and Paul speaks of him as 'my brother.'[20]

Teachers can have proper teacher relationships when they live in the spirit of Paul and Epaphroditus.

Every teacher should be careful not to inadvertantly pass judgment on a fellow worker. If a teacher is not careful, he will be trapped into passing on a critical assessment of a colleague when he has no right to do so. He should remember that students often exaggerate or relate only a portion of what happened in another class. As a result of listening to their stories with too much credulity, a teacher may find himself making an improper evaluation or comment about another. Whether in the personal or professional realm, the teacher should exercise kindness, encouragement, discretion, and care; and the results will be rewarding, not only for the individual, but also for the whole school.

RELATIONSHIP TO PARENTS

If parents did not send their children to Christian schools, there would be no Christian schools. These parents have entrusted their most prized possessions, their children, to the school to be influenced and molded by the teacher; therefore, each teacher has an awesome responsibility both to them and to God.

The instructor should also keep in mind that parents are paying for their children to be taught subject matter, and therefore, deserve to get their money's worth. When students are not taught as they should be, the teacher is not only robbing the parents and cheating the students, but he is also sinning against God.

The Christian teacher should realize that even though he has a great responsibility to parents, the administration has put him in charge of his classroom, and to some degree the teacher is actually acting in the role of the parents in their absence. This role consists of proper teaching, sound discipline, and genuine love and concern for the young people.

Because of the teacher's training and experience, the parents need to accept the teacher's authority in the bounds of the classroom; therefore, the parents should never endeavor to run the classroom or the teacher. Not only are the parents usually less qualified scholastically than the instructor, but they are not familiar with the philosophy and procedures of the school. Their opinions will often be biased by their children's reports on various situations. Such reports are often one-sided and inaccurate on the part of children because of a lack of experience in evaluating problems.

Getting along with parents should be the aim of every teacher, for the child will be the one who suffers if there is a lack of accord between the two authorities.

Smith declares,

All authority comes from God. Those who exercise it toward children must be in harmony with each other. There must be a constant front of unity from both parents and teachers if the child is to grow up with love and respect for authority and discipline.[21]

To ensure this harmony, the teacher should endeavor to have good communication with the parents. If he will learn to "think parents," the instructor will be more effective with his students and their families. By asking himself the following questions, the teacher might avoid some difficulties: for instance, "What would I want to know about this situation if this were my child?" or "Can I justify my doing the following?" or "What might be the parents' reactions to this?" Anticipating parental reaction will often enable a teacher to have a more clear-cut reason for actions that involve academics and discipline.

In conclusion, parents should think of the teacher as their friend and helper. Such an attitude will be easier to have when the teacher is professional and sincere. In addition to these qualities, the following suggestions from Pensocola Christian School are noteworthy:

> Satisfied parents are informed parents. In order for parents to cooperate with us in training their children, communication is important. Follow these guidelines.
> 1. Show concern in a businesslike manner. Be professional, not casual, with parents. Do not give them your first name.
> 2. Suggest ways to solve problems if you can; if you do not know a solution, refer the parent to the Vice Principal.
> 3. Do not apologize for any school policy.
> 4. Do not be pressured by gifts or favors from parents. These are acceptable, but should never influence your training of the student.
> 5. Do not discuss decisions or problems of students with parents unless they directly involve their own children.[22]

RELATIONSHIP TO THE SCHOOL

Every teacher should be loyal to the school where he is laboring for the Lord. One way to develop loyalty is to participate in the various activities such as faculty meetings, athletic events, outings, and other school functions. A person should get involved and enter wholeheartedly into school activities. If nothing is happening, the teacher should try to get something going. Most people require only a little nudge from another person to start worthwhile endeavors.

A teacher can demonstrate his loyalty by always upholding the school; therefore, he should never criticize the place where he works or anyone connected with it. When the Christian worker is loyal to the school, it will be easier for him to teach the young people in his classes to be the same. If at any time another person approaches the teacher to complain about the principal, other teachers, or a school policy, the teacher should take care not to become a party to such criticism. The teacher can avoid becoming part of the problem by referring the disgruntled individual to the one who can best solve the issue.

RELATIONSHIP TO STUDENTS

Because the teacher-student relationship is such a vast field, most of the following material will cover in detail the working of the adult with the students in the classroom.

CONCLUSION

In conclusion, the Christian worker needs to make sure that his relationships are what they should be, for if any of them are neglected, the proper balance with the Lord, with others, and with himself will be affected.

FOOTNOTES

[1]Percy G. Parker, *The Model Christian* (London: Victory Press, 1933), p. 5.

[2]Andrew Murray, *The School of Obedience* (London: Marshall, Morgan and Scott, Ltd., n.d.), p. 16.

[3]Charles Allen, *God's Psychiatry* (Westwood: Fleming H. Revell Co., 1953), p. 17.

[4]G.R. Harding Wood, *Learning and Living the Christian Life* (Roanoke: Progress Press, 1976), p. 25.

[5]C.B. Eavey, *Principles of Teaching for Christian Teachers* (Grand Rapids, Michigan, Zondervan Publishing House, 1971), p. 25.

[6]Matthew 7:29.

[7]Eavey, p. 39.

[8]Ibid., p. 344.

[9]Murray, p. 48.

[10]Eavey, p. 53.

[11]Murray, p. 54.

[12]Ibid., p. 61.

[13]Ronald Schaffer, *Temple Heights Christian School Handbook,* (Tampa, Florida: Temple Heights Baptist Church, 1978). p. 8

[14]V.L. Stanfield, *The Christian Worshipping* (Nashville: Convention Press, 1965), p. 55.

[15]*Institute in Basic Youth Conflicts Syllabus,* (Oak Brook, Ill.), p. 105.

[16]Jack Hyles, *Grace and Truth* (Hammond, Indiana: Hyles-Anderson Pub., 1975), pp. 83-84.

[17]Murray, p. 12.

[18]I Peter 2:14.

[19]I Peter 4:12.

[20]Alan Redpath, *Learning to Live* (Grand Rapids, Mich.: Wm. B. Erdman's Pub. Co., 1962), p. 17.

[21]Thomas Smith, *What Every Parent Should Know about Christian Education* (Murfreesboro, Tenn.: Christian Educator Publications, 1976), p. 56.

[22]*Teacher's Handbook,* Pensacola Christian School, A Beka Publications, p. 28.

QUESTIONS AND PROBLEMS

1. Why are daily private devotions absolutely necessary for the Christian teacher?
2. Why is the Christian teacher's relationship to the Lord so vital?
3. What should the Christian teacher pray for that would make him more effective in the classroom?
4. What would you say is the greatest ability that every teacher should seek from God? The second? The third?
5. Besides the items mentioned in this chapter, what are some other reasons for the teacher to be active and regular in the local church?
6. Why is it a sin against God for a teacher to be unprepared in the presentation of a lesson?
7. Find additional verses of Scripture that apply to the teacher's various relationships at school.
8. Why is proper balance in the various relationships so important for the Christian teacher?

Spiritual Thrust Of The Christian Teacher

Chapter 3

III
SPIRITUAL THRUST OF THE CHRISTIAN TEACHER

"The Christian schools across the United States that are vital, growing, and doing a job for the Lord are those that have a strong evangelistic outreach into the community and a spiritual ministry with their students,"[1] says Baker, vice president of the Pensacola Christian Schools. He goes on to say that the lifeblood and the heartbeat of the Christian school is this evangelistic outreach and spiritual ministry of its people. For this reason, he believes the Lord has given Christian teachers the responsibility to train young people in spiritual matters — whether those youngsters be entrusted to them for "one year, one month, or even one day."[2]

NEED FOR A SPIRITUAL THRUST

The Need to Save the Lost

From the earliest age, the youngster is to be considered a prospect for salvation. While no one should attempt to force a decision upon a child, the Christian teacher must acquaint the child with the fact that he is lost and guilty before a holy, righteous God. By understanding salvation through Christ's atonement, the student can come to know the Lord Jesus as his own personal Savior; he can be freed from his sins to trust in the perfect righteousness of the Son of God.[3]

The Need to Nurture the Saved

The Lord Jesus' commandments, "Feed my lambs . . . feed my sheep,"[4] apply to the servants of God in the classrooms. "Just as a mother

26

needs to select the proper food for a baby and, later, more substantial food for an older child," says Chapman, "so the teacher must select a proper and balanced spiritual diet for the class."[5] Healthy, normal children grow mentally and physically; spiritual babes in Christ should also grow in the grace and knowledge of our Lord Jesus Christ.

The Need to Reach the Students' Relatives

Parents, brothers, sisters, and other relatives of the student are also prospects for discipleship. Every teacher has an open door to visit the home of every pupil, and in the process, to present the plan of salvation to those who do not know Christ as personal Savior. At other times, grandparents, aunts, uncles, and cousins will come to school for special programs, and when relatives come to those occasions, the administration should seize upon the opportunities to witness.[6]

The Need to Be Aware of Immorality

Many parents of young people in Christian schools do not curb their children's TV viewing time, and their youngsters see far too much violence and explicit sex. Moreover, many of these parents do little to restrict the type of music their children listen to or to control the amusements their youngsters indulge in. Such leniency on the part of parents, rather than aiding morality, contributes instead to its corruption. To combat the inconsistencies found between the parents' beliefs and their personal living standards, the Christian teacher must make a determined effort to uphold godliness in and out of the classroom.

CHARACTERISTICS OF THE TEACHER WITH A SPIRITUAL THRUST

The heart of consecration is not devotion to this or that kind of service for Christ; it is devotion to the divine will. It is readiness to do, not what we want to do in Christ's service, but what He gives us to do. When we reach this state of spirit, we shall not need to wait long to find our work.[7]

Called by God

The difference between an occupation and a calling is that the former is pursued in order to earn a living; a calling, on the other hand, is living a life.[8] It is true that when a person works without a calling, he will still accumulate material things, but the servant of God should strive for the spiritual benefits in life. An occupation usually receives from the world; a calling gives to the world. The Christian teacher must be certain that he is giving through Christ; he must have a spiritual thrust to fulfill his calling so that he might have an eternal influence on others.

Controlled by the Holy Spirit

The Holy Spirit will never have a Christian do anything that Christ would not have done in the same situation; therefore, it is the desire of God that His child live a life that is controlled by the Holy Spirit. Such a life will not allow any sin to dominate, for where there is a tolerance of sin, the Holy Spirit will not work through that life.[9]

Lives by Faith

Having faith that God desires to work through him, the Christian teacher will have assurance of the following:

1. He has promised to be with us (Matthew 28:19-20).
2. He has promised us that our work is an eternal one and that our fruit will abide forever (John 15:16).
3. He has promised to bless us here and hereafter (Mark 10:28-30).
4. He has promised to reward us at the Judgment Seat of Christ (Daniel 12:3).[10]

"Faith," says Dr. Pennell of Forrest Hills Baptist Church, "is taking God at His Word, in spite of the circumstances surrounding us. Faith is believing God in spite of your doubts. Belief produces behavior . . .' as a man thinketh in his heart so is he.' "[11]

Maintains a Clean Life Without and Within

A teacher teaches with his life. As Leavitt says, "Your words are important. Your deeds are more important. Your thoughts are most important."[12] R.A. Torrey says,

> If a man is to be used of God his life must be clean — not only his outward life as the world sees it, but his inward secret life as it is known only to God and to himself. One who holds on to any sin or act or thought cannot expect to have power for God. It has often been said, and well said, that "God does not demand a beautiful vessel for His work, but He does demand a clean one."[13]

Motivated by Love

"There is nothing so irresistible as love,"[14] Torrey once pointed out. Indeed, students will not resist a teacher that they really believe loves them; however, they will never believe a teacher loves them unless he really does. The Christian leader must not have a passive feeling for his students but an aggressive commitment to their welfare — a commitment which is motivated by faith. This kind of love is not deterred by students' failure to do what the teacher expects, for Christian love can weather disappointments in the process of leading.[15]

Sustained by Prayer

The Lord desires that His children pray to Him. If they do not, they are not spiritual, for to live a spiritual life means to live a prayerful life. To pray habitually produces godliness, because prayer will strengthen the weak areas, clarify one's spiritual vision, and develop right living. Prayer is to the spiritual nature what breathing is to the physical body. No one can hold his breath and live; neither can a Christian refrain from praying to God and remain spiritually alive.[16]

Is Soul-Conscious

Everybody has a soul, a soul that will spend eternity in heaven or in hell. Because of this fact, every teacher should be very conscious of his students' souls. In addition to that, he should be concerned about the spiritual condition of his students' parents. The Lord Jesus Himself knows the hopelessness of those who are lost, for He said, "The Son of man is come to seek and to save that which was lost" (Luke 19:10). God help Christian teachers to be more soul-conscious in and out of the classroom.

Studies the Bible Daily

In order for the Christian worker to be more effective in his Bible study, he should have a definite time when he gets by himself and reads the Word of God. Probably the best time for private devotions is early in the morning. During that time the teacher can partake of spiritual food from which he will later draw spiritual energy. He should also study the Scriptures at different intervals during the day in order to have a spiritual thrust in every area of his life.

PURPOSE OF THE SPIRITUAL THRUST

Make Students Conscious of Their Needs

Before there is any chance to teach the pupil anything, the teacher must first discover the needs of the youngsters and then make them conscious of their needs.[17] Some of the needs the Christian teacher will bring to the attention of the students are salvation, spiritual growth, witnessing, total surrender, and church involvement. The Christian educator makes definite efforts to show his students their needs, for to do otherwise is sin.

Win the Lost

At the very heart of the teaching-learning process in Christian education is the presentation of Jesus Christ as personal Savior. Of course, it is the Holy Spirit Who must work in the hearts of the young people to show them their need of salvation from their sins through the blood of the Lord Jesus.[18]

Teach Surrender to God

When the truths of God's Word are presented, the pupils should feel constrained to consecrate themselves to Christ and to surrender every area and purpose of their lives to God's will. Eavey says that the Lord Jesus "must be Lord of all if He is to be Lord at all."[19]

Encourage Growth in the New Nature

Whereas the spirit of the old nature cannot understand God's ways, the spirit of the new nature can understand the things of God. Therefore, the Lord begins His work with the new nature, which will love His will and hate sin. He does not do His work all at once, but day by day. Consequently, every student in the class must be encouraged to allow the new nature to grow while he is starving the old nature of sin.

Develop Christian Leadership

The hand of God will not be on every student to give his life in special "full-time" Christian service, but the Christian worker should develop the principles of leadership in all of his students in order that they might help others to know Christ and to grow in Him.[20] There need to be more Christian leaders in every walk of life, such as medicine, law, engineering, politics, industry, and many other fields too numerous to name. God wants His children to make a spiritual impact on the world in all walks of life so that no one will have an excuse not to trust Him as Savior.

HOW TO HAVE A SPIRITUAL THRUST IN THE CLASSROOM

Be a Friend to the Students

At times it would be wise for the teacher to spend some time in conversation with individuals in order to cultivate their friendship and confidence.[21] Rarely do young people confide in someone whom they do not think of as a friend; therefore, the teacher must show his students that he is genuinely interested in their spiritual, social, and academic welfare. Sometimes visiting in the homes of students in one's class helps the students and parents to see the teacher's concern.

Begin the Class with Prayer

The teacher should open every class with prayer. When the teacher prays, three things happen: 1) the teacher asks and believes that God will help him; 2) the students are conscious of the fact that the teacher is depending upon God for his help; and 3) prayer time becomes an opportunity for the teacher and students to share one another's burdens. If the instructor believes that "Prayer changes things," he can trust God that things will be different because he has prayed.

Integrate the Bible with All Subject Matter

Every time an occasion affords itself, the teacher should seize the opportunity to apply a Bible truth or principle. The Lord desires to be included in every aspect of teaching, and He will be if the teacher looks for ways to incorporate godly precepts into every discipline. Joseph Gettys believes that "When the Bible itself is used as a basic resource, it feeds its life into other studies to enrich them and to make them more receptive."[22]

Teach a Wide Range of Truth

Goodman says that some teachers never get further than, "You are a sinner; God loves you; Christ died for you; believe and you will be saved."[23] These teachings are wonderfully true, but to repeat them endlessly will not enable the young Christian to grow as he should. The youngsters must be exposed to much more, because the glories of Christ are endless. Indeed, declares Goodman, "The whole counsel of God should be declared so that Christian character can be formed. The word Gospel is not limited in its meaning to the way a sinner can be justified, but it includes all good news from heaven."[24]

Make Applications on the Level of the Pupils

"Applications must be made, of course," Rozell reminds us, "on the age level and the spiritual plane of the pupils. The applications chosen and the manner in which they are phrased will depend upon the age of the pupils."[25] Most every teacher realizes that small children have different needs and receive applications in a different manner from that in which teenagers receive them. The teacher should also consider the spiritual level of each student, and he should not expect the same response from a young Christian as he would from someone who is more spiritually mature. Practical, relevant applications drawn from the students' everyday lives are always helpful and pertinent.[26]

Expose the Students to Sound, Biblical Music

All too often in Christian schools, the students are not taught to appreciate the great hymns of the faith. If there is any singing at all on the part of the pupils, it is frothy, rhythmical ditties that appeal primarily to the feet and not to the heart. However, says Goodman, "Hymns well chosen are a great storehouse of truth and have in many cases been used in after years to bring conviction and lead to repentance."[27]

CONCLUSION

Baker writes, "Public education has failed! It is failing to provide a good academic education while exposing our children to a godless, secular-humanistic approach to life."[28] In addition to this failure, secular schools are also failing to provide a spiritual thrust that is required for young people to have a God-fearing, God-honoring approach to life based upon the Holy Scriptures. Without the daily commitment of surrendered teachers, Christian schools will be no better than the public schools, and it is the teachers in the classrooms that determine what kind of a godly ministry the schools have. Certainly the Lord Jesus Christ Himself desires that every school that bears the name "Christian" have a spiritual thrust that would bring honor and glory to His name.

FOOTNOTES

[1]A.A. Baker, *The Successful Christian School* (Pensacola, Florida: A Beka Book Publications, 1979), p. 23.

[2]Ibid., p. 24.

[3]C.B. Eavey, "Aims and Objectives of Christian Education," *An Introduction to Evangelical Christian Education*, edited by J. Edward Hakes (Chicago: Moody Press 1964), p. 62.

[4]John 21:15, 17.

[5]Marie M. Chapman, *Practical Methods for Sunday School Teachers* (Grand Rapids, Mich.: Zondervan Pub. House, 1962), p. 9.

[6]Guy P. Leavitt, *Teach with Success* (Cincinnati, Ohio: Standard Publishing, 1956), p. 34.

[7]J.R. Miller, *The Building of Character* (London: The Sunday School Union, n.d.), p. 52.

[8]Clarence H. Benson, *The Sunday School in Action* (Chicago: Moody Press, 1953), p. 324.

[9]William W. Pennell, *Church Leadership Seminar* (Decatur, Georgia: Forrest Hills Baptist Church) pp. 9-10.

[10]Tom Malone, *Essentials of Evangelism* (Murfreesboro, Tennessee: Sword of the Lord Publishers, 1958), pp. 91-92.

[11]William W. Pennell, "Faith," Sunday School Lesson, Forrest Hills Baptist Church, Decatur, Georgia. (Mimeograph)

[12]Leavitt, p. 13.

[13]R.A. Torrey, *Personal Work* (Westwood, N.J.: Fleming H. Revell Company, n.d.), p. 15.

[14]Ibid., p. 17.

[15]Kenneth O. Gangel, *Leadership for Church Education* (Chicago: Moody Press, 1970), p. 176.

[16]Benson, p. 321.

[17]Ray Rozell, *Talks on Sunday School Teaching* (Grand Rapids, Michigan: Zondervan Publishing House, 1969), p. 43.

[18]H.W. Byrne, *Christian Education for the Local Church* (Grand Rapids, Michigan: Zondervan Publishing House, 1969), p. 248.

[19]Eavey, p. 62.

[20]Kenneth O. Gangel, *Understanding Teaching* (Wheaton, Illinois: Evangelical Teacher Training Association, 1968), p. 26.

[21]Benson, p. 158.

[22]Joseph M. Gettys, *How to Teach the Bible* (Richmond, Virginia: John Knox Press, 1966), p. 11.

[23]George Goodman, *What To Teach and How To Teach the Young* (London: Pickering and Inglis Ltd., 1946), p. 5.

[24]Ibid.

[25]Rozell, p. 100.

[26]Anthony C. Deane, *Jesus Christ* (London: Hodder and Stoughton, 1935), p. 69.

[27]Goodman, p. 4.

[28]Baker, p. 16.

QUESTIONS AND PROBLEMS

1. Why do you think that many teachers in Christian schools do not have a spiritual impact upon their pupils?

2. Is the teacher at fault if young people do not respond in a spiritual way?

3. Should every graduate from a Christian school be a Christian? Why?

4. In what grade should the plan of salvation be presented? Should every teacher be responsible for presenting the plan of salvation?

5. What if a student and his parents do not think the subject of Bible is important and care little if the subject is failed?

6. Should Christian schools have non-believers come in to explain their positions to the students? Why?

7. Are graduates of a Christian school indicative of what the school is like?

8. Do you think it is right for a teacher to discuss biblical issues in classes other than Bible class? Give reasons to support your answer.

Teaching Character

Chapter 4

IV
TEACHING CHARACTER

In politics, in the ministry, and in business there is a desperate need for people who have character. Personality is important; talent is important; but a good personality with talent will oftentimes run from character. The motto of some seems to be, "Why work hard? I have it made. I can talk my way out of it." On the other hand, a child that is taught to have character will get the necessary talent. Talent oftentimes flees character. Character will always seek talent — that is, the talent necessary to fulfill the task. How vital it is that we stress character and place each of its qualities in the proper order.[1]

Dr. Bob Jones, Sr., said, "Your character is what God knows you to be. Your reputation is what men think you are."[2] Again he said, "The test of your character is what you would do if you knew no one would ever know."[3] Character, then, has to do with whether a person chooses to do right or wrong, and his attitude will determine those choices. From the Christian point of view, morality and a personal relationship with God are inseparable in the forming of character.

Not only are the home and church involved in the process of forming and molding values in the lives of young people, but the school is also instrumental in developing character. Character, according to Fremont, is the fashioning of "permanent beliefs which result in consistent behavior patterns . . . those patterns are established by the age of twenty."[4] Thus it is evident how important the development of character is during the school years.

HOW CHARACTER IS FORMED

Character is formed by a variety of minute circumstances, more or less under the control and regulation of the individual. Some of those circumstances are good and some are bad; however, there is nothing too small or trivial in building character in one's life.

Shaping of the Will

Berry says that the will of a child is made of steel. From birth it is full of strength and is able to express itself.[5] Dobson believes the will must be molded and shaped, for it is the training and the bending of the child's will that enables him to learn to yield to authority.[6] And thus, a child will learn to yield to God by yielding to the authority of his parents and teachers.[7]

The tested experience of the adult assists him in shaping the youngster's will so that the child might become a better person. In order for that to happen, the student must trust the teacher to help him or her. Smiles puts it this way:

> As in school, many of the lessons learned there must needs be taken on trust. We may not understand them, and may possibly think it hard that we have to learn them, especially where the teachers are trials, sorrows, temptations, and difficulties; and yet we must not only accept their lessons, but recognize them as being divinely appointed.[8]

The teacher must be in control; his authority must be accepted. Discipline and authority in school make the child's world understandable, for if the teacher does not guide the youngster in his decisions, the burden of the child becomes too great. Hein says, "The child learns eventually that, although the pursuit of happiness is guaranteed to him, it is not achieved without accepting discipline and responsibility."[9] As a result, he learns that by submitting his will to the person in charge, his right to be free is guaranteed only within the limits set by the teacher. He will also learn that acceptance of basic responsibilities will bring happiness into his life.[10]

Breaking the child's will should never be confused with breaking a young person's spirit, for the spirit of a youngster is his ego or his self-worth. Every person should have pride in himself — not an arrogant pride that makes him think he is better than others, but a respect for himself as an individual who has been created to glorify God.

Building on the Word of God

Miller insists that lasting character must be built on God's pattern for one's life, and a person can discover in the Bible every aspect of God's pattern. The precepts of Christ, the teachings of the apostles, and the lives of the godly are all models for character formation. These great eternal principles found in the Word of God should be the basis for character training in the Christian school.[11] Absolute truth, which can be found only in the Bible, presents three unchangeable principles of character: truth, purity, and love. Unless these are a part of the superstructure of his life, the individual builds in vain.

Conforming to Christ

The ideals and standards of many persons change with every new philosophy introduced by men; yet God's standard has never changed, for God's ultimate standard is to be like Christ. Eavey writes, " Christ is the standard of personal conduct."[12] In Christ the believer discovers a life truly submitted to the will of God. "Christ's character is the model, the ideal, for every Christian life."[13]

Yielding to the Holy Spirit

Christian character is produced by the Holy Spirit, not by human effort. Such character is not a matter of legal or moral correctness, rather it is the possession and the manifestation of nine qualities which the Holy Spirit creates in the believer. Eavey elaborates,

> These outcomes of the Spirit's working are love, joy, and peace — character as a state of the heart; patience, kindness, and goodness — character as expressed in contacts with fellow men; faithfulness, gentleness, and self-control — character directed Godward.[14]

The Lord has given the Holy Spirit to every believer so that he might be freed from the blight and corruption of self-will, and by yielding to the Spirit of God, the Christian can choose the best way of life. But, as C.B. Eavey explains, "The Christian teacher cannot assume that, because teaching which is Christian is done by the Spirit of God, there is nothing for him to do."[15] The teacher must, Eavey says,

> Trust in God but be prepared by way of getting yourself in tune with God and by way of mastering all the knowledge you can about human nature, the content of teaching, and the principles and techniques of teaching. To be a good Christian teacher, he must labor to obtain the best he can in preparation for his great work and for doing it through the years. But his trust while doing the work is in God, not in his knowledge of the ways of teaching.[16]

Making the Effort

Smiles believes that no matter how much an individual may desire good character, he cannot achieve it without effort. He needs to strive constantly to be temperate, self-disciplined, and discreet. Though at times he may stumble and fall and experience temporary defeat, if his spirit is strong and his heart submissive to God, he will ultimately succeed.

The very effort to arrive at a higher standard of character is inspiring and satisfying, and even though the Christian may fall short of his goal, he cannot fail to improve by his honest effort.[17] Each person must make the effort to build his own character because no one else can do it for him. Every person must choose on his own to be pure or impure, true or false, humble or proud, trustworthy or deceitful; the character of an individual is fashioned by himself.[18]

Forming Proper Habits

Every decision a person makes helps to develop some habit — whether it be good or bad; thus, as Eavey explains, character is nothing more than the development of habits.[19] Proper living does not happen by accident. In fact, he says, "There is one way, and only one way to fashion a moral character and that is to hammer and to shape it into being on the hard anvil of daily living."[20] Hyles adds that after doing right consciously for a long period of time, a person comes to do right subconsciously because his reflexes take over, and when that occurs, the character habit is established.[21]

FACTORS IN TEACHING CHARACTER

Example

When a teacher incorporates principles in his instruction, he must put these principles into practice before he can expect his students to do so. His example, then, becomes an important key in developing his students' character. The example of godly teachers is indeed the most important influence at the disposal of the school for the building of character. Everything that a teacher does affects the students in some way because of his continual contact with them.[22] Thus, the teacher has the responsibility of demonstrating good character. Character traits are caught as well as taught, and much teaching has been negated because the teacher is not a living example of what he teaches.[23]

Fear

A teacher can avoid many difficulties in character training by teaching a young person to fear the Lord, for as Proverbs 8:13a declares, "The fear of the Lord is to hate evil." Ecclesiastes 12:13 says, "Fear God, and keep His commandments: for this is the whole duty of man." Fearing God will encourage a person to do right, since "The fear of the Lord is the beginning of knowledge" (Proverbs 1:7a).

May contends that when the adult in charge establishes a punishment for wrong behavior, he instills an element of fear into the hearts of his students; however, his punishments should be administered with care, concern, and sympathetic understanding so that the end result is a reinforcement of the proper ties between the teacher and the pupil.[24] By demanding accountability and responsibility from children, the teacher will develop successful young people.[25]

Motivation

One of the most positive motivating factors in teaching is love. A teacher who loves his students and who is loved in return is pretty sure to influence them. Indeed, as Hughes puts it, "Development in Christian character is in some senses growth in love."[26]

Still another motivating factor promoting character in the lives of pupils is the knowledge that they are making progress. "The praise and commendation of a respected teacher," says Eavey, "often spurs a pupil on to more intense effort and greater achievements."[27]

Standards

Secular society with its relative values offers little for anyone except doing his own thing, but, thank God, in the Bible a Christian can find real guidance and standards.[28] The standards established by the Christian school must be based on the Word of God, for there is no greater Absolute. When there are infractions of these Biblical standards, it is the student who must adjust his ways so that proper attitudes will be attained. By achieving a proper attitude, he will not only grow in character, but he will make things more pleasant for those around him.

TEACHING CHARACTER IN THE CLASSROOM

After the influence of the home, the school is probably the greatest influence in the youngster's life. It is in the school environment that the teacher's influence is so important, for the child will spend as much time with the teacher as with the parent. The classroom, therefore, becomes one of the greatest potentials for the development of proper character in the life of the student. The following are ways that the teacher may teach character in the classroom:

Show the Need of Character

One of the best motivational factors for teaching anything is to see the need of something; therefore, the student should be shown the need for character. The student should understand that the end result of doing right will produce satisfaction in his life "whenever it satifies some need he feels, provides some value he wants, supplies some control he wishes to possess, secures some desired end, or helps him to attain any definite goal."[29] Therefore, it is more important for the pupil to learn the need of being what he should be rather than what he should know. Smith says, "Character teaching is teaching the child to be honest, hard-working, and respectful of others. If a child learns what he should be, then he will learn what he should know."[30]

Have Classroom Standards of Conduct

Eavey believes that "Schools are habit factories."[31] Christian habits are the result of Christian instruction; therefore, the teacher must of necessity establish standards of conduct that will produce godly character. "If pupils are not forming right habits of proper behavior and politeness, they are inevitably forming habits of inattention, heedlessness, wrong behavior, and rudeness."[32] The classroom where pupils are permitted to be loud, disobedient, discourteous, and disruptive is doing the young people more harm than good, and the students are developing habits that will hinder them later in life.

The teacher's love for the students does not refrain him from administering discipline. Eavey continues, "Love looks to the end result and uses correction, reproof, instruction, punishment, or anything else, unpleasant though it be, if it gives promise of bringing about the outcome desired."[33] And that outcome is obedience to the rules and regulations set down by the teacher. Rules and regulations teach that obedience with a proper attitude is important for the formation of character. Murray sums it up simply when he says, "Obedience is the one certificate of Christian character."[34]

Develop Standards through Classroom Responsibilities

Every recitation and every lesson gives the Christian teacher an opportunity to build character into the lives of his pupils. The instructor needs to stress the importance of the students' finishing what they start, doing their work neatly, and finding other things to do when their work is finished. Young people should learn the importance of paying attention, taking care of their materials, recognizing the good in each one's contributions, and accepting criticism. In addition to these things, the teacher should guide the young people in sharing things with others, taking turns, doing their share of the work, taking part in the lesson, and respecting the feelings of others.[35]

Koehler concludes by saying,

> Children should apply themselves diligently to their tasks and do their work carefully, neatly, conscientiously. They must be held to do at all times the best they can under the circumstances and never be satisfied with slipshod work. We must encourage them in their work, acknowledge their diligence and their progress, show them how to improve, etc. Thus we must lead them on to greater efforts and to greater achievements, directing the natural instinct to be busy into useful activity.[36]

Teach Character through Academics

Through academic subjects, students should be challenged to form godly thoughts and responses. Attitudes are formed by requiring all students to complete the assignments on time and according to the directions given by the instructor. Character is taught when teachers encourage the pupils to try their best, to follow directions, to develop orderliness, to do right regardless of the consequences.

Encourage Pupils in the Classroom

Teachers need to encourage students to do great things, for encouragement will change ordinary lives into great and useful individuals.[37] A patient teacher does not expect miracles overnight, but he will encourage his pupils with kind and sympathetic words. Students know when a teacher desires that they achieve in every area of their lives because the teacher's attitude cannot be hidden, and as a result, changes take place in the attitudes of the young people.

Incorporate God's Word into Everything

Probably the most important way of instilling character in the lives of the pupils is to incorporate the Bible into every aspect of the classroom. Verses of Scripture should be applied to every subject; in short, the Word of God should be integrated into every experience during the class day. Every event in the classroom has a purpose when the Word of God is properly applied by the Holy Spirit because God's Word is powerful, and He desires to have its principles appropriated.

Teach through Constant Training

Finally, Hicks has developed certain principles that need to be constantly remembered by the teacher to ensure that character training is achieved. These principles are: 1) the young people must understand the principles of character in order to produce deliberated actions; 2) pupils should learn to do right because it is right to do right; 3) the students should see that honesty works; 4) a great deal of life is painful and restrictive, and therefore, the young people should be required to "endure some things that do not produce immediate gratification";[38] 5) the students' wills have to be trained; 6) the pupils need to be trained daily through the Scriptures; and 7) young people should be encouraged to use character principles so that they will make proper decisions on their own after they leave the influence of the school.[39]

CONCLUSION

The aim of the Christian teacher is "that the man of God may be perfect, throughly furnished unto all good works" (II Timothy 3:17). "All of Christian teaching is directed to the one final and only aim of the up-building of those taught in perfection of godly character,"[40] says Eavey. Thus, the key to Biblical Christian character is simply trusting God and doing right.

FOOTNOTES

[1]Jack Hyles, *Blue Denim and Lace* (Hammond, Indiana: Hyles Anderson Publishers, 1969), p. 45.

[2]Eleanor L. Doan, *The Speaker's Sourcebook* (Grand Rapids: Zondervan Publishing House, 1971), p. 46.

[3]Ibid.

[4]Walter G. Fremont, "Building Character in Youth," *Balance* (Greenville, SC: Bob Jones University Press), p. 1.

[5]Ray Berry, *Practical Child Training* (Pleasant Hill, Ohio: The Parents Association Publishers, n.d.), p. 1451.

[6]James Dobson, *Dare to Discipline* (New York: Bantam Books, 1970), p. 87.

[7]Ibid., p. 88.

[8]Samuel Smiles, *Character* (New York: A.L. Burt, Publishers, n.d.), p. 348.

[9]Lucille Hein, *Enjoy Your Children* (New York: Abingdon Press, 1959), p. 211.

[10]Ibid.

[11]J.R. Miller, *The Building of Character* (London: The Sunday School Union, n.d.), p. 26.

[12]C.B. Eavey, *Principles of Teaching for Christian Teachers* (Grand Rapids: Zondervan Publishing House, 1940), pp. 115-116.

[13]Miller, p. 26.

[14]Eavey, pp. 115-116.

[15]C.B. Eavey, *Principles of Christian Ethics* (Grand Rapids, Michigan: Zondervan Publishing House, 1958), p. 60.

[16]Ibid.

[17]Smiles, p. 22.

[18]Miller, p. 11.

[19]Eavey, *Principles of Teaching,* p. 65.

[20]Eavey, *Principles of Christian Ethics,* p. 119.

[21]Jack Hyles, Sermon on "Character" as printed in *Rebirth of Our Nation* Accelerated Christian Education, 1979.

[22]Harry C. McKnown, *Character Education* (New York: Mcgraw-Hill Book Company, Inc., 1935), pp. 303-304.

[23]Walter G. Fremont, "Christian Character Development," *Voice of the Alumni,* April 1973, Bob Jones University, Greenville, South Carolina.

[24]Philip May, *Which Way to Educate?* (Chicago: Moody Press, 1975), p. 146.

[25]James Dobson, *Hide or Seek* (Old Tappen, N.J.: Fleming H. Revell Co., 1974), p. 82.

[26]H. Trevor Hughes, *Faith and Life* (London: Cox and Wyman, Ltd., 1962), p. 33.

[27]C.B. Eavey, *The Art of Effective Teaching* (Grand Rapids, Michigan: Zondervan Publishing House, 1940), p. 143.

[28]Milford Sholund, "Teaching Junior High School Youth," An Introduction to Evangelical Christian Education, edited by J. Edward Hakes (Chicago: Moody Press, 1972), p. 180.

[29]McKnown, p. 289.

[30]Thomas Smith, What Every Parent Should Know About Christian Education (Murfreesboro: The Christian Educator Pub., 1976), p. 39.

[31]Eavey, Principles for Teaching, p. 65.

[32]Ibid.

[33]Eavey, Teaching Christian Ethics, p. 275.

[34]Andrew Murray, The School of Obedience (London: Marshall, Morgan and Scott, Ltd., n.d.), pp. 19-20.

[35]Eavey, The Art . . . , p. 16.

[36]Edward A Koehler, A Christian Pedagogy (New Ulm, Minn.: Martin Albrecht Publisher, 1930), p. 238.

[37]Gilbert Highet, The Art of Teaching (New York: Alfred A. Knopf Pub., 1973), p. 154.

[38]Laurel Hicks, "Character Training vs. Behavior Modification," as quoted in A.A. Baker, The Successful Christian School (Pensacola, Florida: A Beka Book Publications, 1979), p. 202.

[39]Ibid., pp. 201-202.

[40]Eavey, Principles of Teaching . . . , p. 54.

QUESTIONS AND PROBLEMS

1. Do you think that most Christian schools are producing young people with Christian character? Support your answer.
2. Can a teacher who does not possess character teach character? Why?
3. What do you consider to be the greatest character trait? What is the second? What is the third?
4. When you think of character, who comes to your mind? Why do you think of that person as one having strong character?
5. Who is your favorite Old Testament individual who had great character? Explain. Who is your favorite New Testament character?
6. Can a Christian school develop character in a student's life if the parents of that student are weak in character? Explain.
7. What part should fear play in the development of character? Who do young people fear?
8. How will the following things develop character in the lives of teachers and students?

    Reading the Bible   Giving the tithe
    Attending church   Praying
    Soul winning   Studying lessons

Classroom Control/Discipline

Chapter 5

V
CLASSROOM CONTROL/DISCIPLINE

A teacher may be a very spiritual person, and that same teacher may excel in his knowledge of the academic material; but if he cannot control young people in his classroom, they will not be able to benefit from what he has to offer. In short, everything else goes out the window.

Richard Kindsuatter contends that classroom management is essential because "without a favorable classroom climate very little teaching or learning will occur."[1] He also believes that there is a close relationship between the management of children and the influence on them. Therefore, the problem of discipline becomes a crucial factor for every teacher.

The career of many a potentially fine teacher has become shipwrecked over the issue of control. "While good disciplinarians are not necessarily excellent teachers, excellent teachers are necessarily good disciplinarians in the enlightened sense of the word."[2]

In almost every poll of people concerned about education, the problem of discipline usually ranks first on the lists; however, most secular educators approach the subject with great caution and some fear because they regard discipline as mere negative reinforcement. As a result of this self-imposed blind spot, a crisis in the area of classroom management has developed in most secular schools and some Christian programs. Indeed, despite the wealth of courses offered in teacher training programs, one might be hard-pressed to discover even two schools that offer a course on "Discipline" or "Classroom Control."

Jones relates the following:

> Teachers repeatedly express to me their bitterness at not having
> been prepared in their course work and student teaching to deal effec-
> tively with the frequent student misbehavior that is commonplace in
> almost any classroom. At best, a few simplistic behavioral techniques
> were covered briefly in some programs, but most teachers report that
> when they raised the issue with their professors, they were told they
> would "pick it up on the job."[3]

But do teachers "pick it up on the job"? If they fail to acquire this
most essential component of instruction, what is the resulting loss?

Dobson declares,

> It has been estimated that 80% of the teachers who quit their
> jobs after the first year do so because of an inability to maintain
> discipline in their classrooms. Do the colleges and teacher training
> programs respond to this need of offering specific courses in methods
> of control? No! Do the State Legislatures require formal course work
> to help teachers handle this first prerequisite to teaching? No, despite
> the fact that learning is impossible in a chaotic classroom.[4]

In most instances, discipline in Christian schools is quite different
from that in secular institutions. The outgrowth of correction that the
Christian seeks is the development of character — a change in the attitude, the actions, and the thinking of students. The purpose behind the
use of punishment and correction is to guide a student in the paths of
righteousness. This approach is contrary to the philosophy of the Progres-
sive/Humanists. Humanism is man-centered, whereas "the Christian philosophy of education is Christ-controlled, pupil-related, Bible-integrated,
and socially applied."[5]

Control is usually obtained very easily by teachers who establish
"fair and appropriate rules; who are consistent in what they say; who say
only what they really mean; and who regularly follow up with appropriate
action whenever necessary."[6] Good discipline, thus, will result in a relaxed,
happy, and satisfying atmosphere.

"The key to good discipline is the teacher,"[7] declares Thelma
Johnson. She believes that the teacher's attitude towards the students
and the academic material produces positive results:

> The class reflects the teacher. If she is organized, they will be. If
> she is quiet, they will be. If she is enthusiastic, they will be. There will
> be fewer discipline problems in a classroom that is organized, quiet,
> and enthusiastic.
>
> The character and success of a class will be determined in a large
> part by its operating standards. These standards are the rules or

boundaries . . . The boundaries will be challenged and tested by the students. At this strategic point, the teacher determines (portrays) the importance of the boundary by stopping the behavior of the student and either correcting his direction through re-explanation or through appropriate punishment.

However, once proven, these same boundary lines serve as security to the children, allowing them appropriate freedom within their boundaries. They want to be shown, want to be given a clear understanding of what is expected from them. Through the use of boundaries, they learn respect and obedience. Many factors contribute to the enjoyment of a child's freedom within boundaries.[8]

REASONS FOR LACK OF CONTROL AND POOR DISCIPLINE

There are many reasons a teacher may lack control of his class. The cause may be only one of the following or a combination of several; at any rate, the Christian teacher should take care to avoid such entrapments.

The Teacher May Lack the Concept That God Has Placed Him in That Classroom

Many Christian teachers do not have an awareness that it is God Who has placed them in the classroom to manage those special young people. By means of the administration, the Lord Himself has designated a specific instructor for a group of children. Each teacher must understand that God has made him accountable for his group and that no one else can do the work that he has been given. "He [the teacher] must be convinced that God has placed him there [in the classroom] and will speak through him with authority. He must realize he is representing Christ."[9]

The Teacher May Be Afraid of a Student or Students

Some teachers are psychologically intimidated by their students. However, teachers who allow young people to be disrespectful and to disrupt the class lack courage. They are cowards who surrender their responsibilities to subordinates usurping a position that is not theirs. To the fearful teacher the Bible declares, "For God has not given us the spirit of fear, but power, and love, and a sound mind" (II Timothy 1:7). Again the Word of God states, "The Lord is on my side; I will not fear: what can man do unto me?" (Psalm 118:6).

The Teacher May Desire to Be Liked by Students

Perhaps one of the biggest problems first year teachers have in the matter of discipline is that they want to be liked by their pupils.

"I wanted them to like me," confessed a first year teacher who was having a great deal of difficulty controlling his class. Schain and Polner report that this type of trouble is not uncommon with young, new teachers.[10] A person might ask, "But isn't it normal and natural to want the students to like you?" and the answer is "Yes." However, that should not be the primary goal of any teacher — especially not of the Christian teacher, for he has the Lord Jesus Christ as his example. Did Christ come to this earth to be liked? The answer is "No." In John 5:30 Christ declared, "I seek not Mine own will, but the will of the Father Who hath sent Me."

In other words, just as the Lord came to do the will of the Father, the Christian teacher goes into the classroom with his primary motive to do the will of the Father. The Christian should do God's will whether he is "liked" or not. "Remember that your job is that of teacher," Marsha Rudman points out. "Don't let your overwhelming desire to make the children love you get in your way. You have a responsibility beyond affection."[11]

The Teacher May Not Analyze His Discipline Problems

From time to time the teacher should stop and analyze deviant situations. He may discover the same patterns of misconduct happening under particular circumstances. An awareness of these patterns should enable the teacher to make any necessary adjustments before such problems occur. Because the teacher is the key to any classroom problems, he must endeavor to avoid or to correct discipline difficulties. The Christian has the advantage over others in that he is able to seek God's help and trust the Holy Spirit to analyze his problems.

The Teacher May Not Be Prepared

According to Walter E. McPhie, one of the main reasons a teacher has discipline problems is that he is not thoroughly prepared. Preparation of one's lessons has a tremendous effect on discipline. According to McPhie, any instructor who is thoroughly prepared knows the following:

> 1) What he hopes to achieve during any given lesson and how this daily effort relates to the larger goals; 2) Why his lesson is important; 3) How he intends to teach the lesson; and 4) What materials or aids will be needed in the process. A detailed treatment of lesson planning may be found readily elsewhere, but a few paragraphs of basic information at the teacher's fingers will help to establish a relationship between preparation and behavior problems.[12]

A competent teacher has work on hand for the young people to do at all times. Having work on hand does not mean busy work, which is deadly, but it does mean work of value that the children will find challenging.

The Teacher May Lack an Interest in His Work

If the teacher lacks interest in what he is teaching, he can expect the same from his pupils; and when the young people are not interested, they will discover other means to divert their attention. When the latter happens, the teacher reaps discipline problems for himself. Not only that, the disinterested teacher does irreparable harm to himself by settling for mediocrity in his own life. He not only fails to inspire others, but he becomes tranquilized by his own lack of interest, and he is the greatest loser of all.

The Teacher Is Not Backed by the Administration

Most Christian school administrators uphold the teachers in discipline matters as much as they possibly can. By supporting the teacher's authority, an effective principal enables the Christian worker not to lose face. Upholding a teacher's authority does not imply covering up a miscarriage of justice, nor should the principal avoid dealing with such a problem. The skillful administrator handles the incident in such a wise way that the difficulty is corrected while the superstructure of the teacher's authority has not been destroyed.

Some school administrators are the last to admit that they do not back their teachers when discipline problems arise. However, their lack of support is often due to fear of board members, parents, or students. Strong principals serve as "a role model for both students and teachers" when they institute a firm, fair, and consistent system of discipline.[13] However, since not all administrators will assume such a role model, teachers need to make sure the administration is with them before they get out on a limb.

RESULTS OF POOR DISCIPLINE

The "Cause and Effect" principle is very evident in the area of discipline. The Bible declares, ". . . whatsoever a man soweth, that shall he also reap" (Galatians 6:7b). When the teacher sows the correct principles of control, those principles will produce the desired respect, learning, and character in his students. On the other hand, the poor disciplinarian encourages disrespect, indifferent performance, and lack of character. The results of a lack of control in the classroom will be demonstrated in the following areas:

Poor Discipline Hinders Learning

"We know the amount and quality of teaching are directly affected by the habits we develop within our students,"[14] says Barbara Bradley. Indeed, when young people are disruptive, they not only miss the instruction themselves, but they also distract others and make learning more difficult for those around them. Therefore, the Christian teacher must instill in his students suitable habits of listening, of following directions, and of achieving in order to facilitate learning.

The teacher is the key to the transmission of learning to the students. "Every teacher must have control of what is going on in the classroom . . . and this cannot be done when they [the pupils] are not paying attention and when the resulting climate is chaotic."[15]

Lack of Control Hinders the Overall School Program

A school is like the body of a human being: there are various parts with differing functions. When one part of the body is weak, it hinders the maximum operations of the whole body. The same is true of a school situation. Every worker must do his part to maintain appropriate discipline so that the overall program does not suffer. DeZafra says,

> Not only is good discipline imperative for the establishment and development of the successful teacher's career, but it is also imperative to the success of the school. Education cannot proceed without good discipline. Youngsters encouraged to lawlessness by one weak teacher make the work of their other teachers just that much more difficult.[16]

Parents Lose Faith in the School

Children usually tell their parents about the teacher who does not handle discipline problems properly. After hearing the stories their children tell, the parents often begin to feel that they are being cheated because their children do not receive adequate instruction while in that teacher's class. The school then loses good public relations with the parents.

The "Easy Way" Becomes the "Hard Way"

During the course of a school year, all of the uncontrolled deviate problems take their toll. If at first the teacher overlooks the minor infractions of misconduct of one or two, as time goes on, others begin to act the same way. Soon minor problems evolve into greater distractions. Even though on some days there may not be any major behavioral problems, the overall continuous correcting of pupils will cause the teacher to feel wiped out. A teacher can plan only so many lessons and watch them wasted on half the class before instructing begins to look futile to him.[17]

Poor Discipline Weakens the Character of Young People

The Word of God admonishes the Christian worker to instill "good works" into the lives of those that are under him.

> Put them in mind to be subject to principalities and powers, to obey magistrates, to be ready to every good work. To speak evil of no man, to be no brawlers, but gentle, showing all meekness unto all men.
> And let ours also learn to maintain good works for necessary uses, that they be not unfruitful (Titus 3:1, 2, 14).

Every Christian teacher should be convinced that "good works" on the part of his students make them fruitful, while bad behavior produces unproductive lives. The leader should have a plan by which he might achieve suitable attitudes. Dobson asks the following questions:

Have you consciously examined the values which you are teaching to your children? Are you following a well-conceived plan on their behalf, instilling attitudes and concepts which are worthy of their dedication? The human spirit must have something meaningful in which to believe, and the instructional responsibility is much too important to handle in a haphazard manner.[18]

Conscientious Young People Do Not Like Weak Teachers

Down deep inside, every young person desires to be a success in life; he wants to be equipped with the necessary skills that will enable him to accomplish his goals. He is aware of being cheated by weak teachers who cannot control the class when they are teaching. Some teachers even think that their pupils like them for being easy on them, but in actuality, the young people hold them in disrespect and make fun of them behind their backs. Again Dobson points out,

When a class is out of control, particularly at the elementary school level, the children are afraid of each other. If the teacher can't make the class behave, how can she prevent a bully from doing his thing? How can she keep the students from laughing at one of its less able members? Children are not very fair and understanding with each other, and they feel good about having a strong teacher who is.[19]

It may seem strange, but youngsters appreciate teachers who are demanding in their discipline. "Children admire strict teachers because chaos is nerve-wracking. Screaming and hitting are fun for about ten minutes; then the confusion begins to get tiresome and irritating."[20]

PURPOSE OF GODLY DISCIPLINE

The Bible gives us the purpose of discipline in Job 36:10-11.

He openeth also their ear to discipline, and commandeth that they return from iniquity. If they obey and serve Him, they shall spend their days in prosperity and their years in pleasures.

By having a godly, disciplined life, an individual deals with sin (iniquity) in his own life and in the area around him. When he obeys and serves the Lord by the control of the Holy Spirit, then the Christian enjoys prosperity and pleasures.

Discipline without a purpose is like traveling without a destination; however, the effective teacher has definite purposes with godly discipline. Those purposes are:

To Demonstrate the Work of the Holy Spirit

Many teachers work for years and years having good control in the classroom, but they neglect the real Spirit of discipline. They control their classes, but their results are through the energy of the flesh because they do not yield themselves to the Holy Spirit every day. However, when a teacher surrenders himself daily to the Spirit of God, God will work through him, and the results will be seen in the lives of the students. Smith believes, "The Holy Spirit is the only true disciplinarian. He is the spirit of discipline."[21]

To Bring about a Change in Behavior

Not only is it necessary for students to correct improper behavior, but in those corrections the young people must learn to improve and to change their ways of life. Schaefer says, "The goal of punishment and discipline is to teach children to develop their own inner controls."[22] Many times students conform to the rules placed over them, but when they are taken out of that environment, they drop such restrictions and revert to their old ways. If external discipline does not produce internal discipline, something is wrong.

To Teach Submission to Authority

God's Word commands, "Obey them that have the rule over you, and submit yourselves: for they watch for your souls, as they that must give account" (Hebrews 13:17). No one can be a productive Christian until he is willing to obey the authority that he sees; for if an individual is not submissive to the authority that he sees, he will not be submissive to the Authority of God Whom he does not see. Consequently, the Christian teacher has a spiritual obligation to encourage the students to yield to his direction. A child's willful resistance to the control of the teacher is an indication that the youngster is resisting the power of God over his life. For the benefit of the child, that willfulness must be dealt with.

To Curb Unrighteousness

The Bible clearly states that unrighteousness should be dealt with for the sake of those who want to do right. "When the scorner is punished, the simple is made wise; and when the wise is instructed, he receiveth knowledge."[23] Curbing unrighteousness in the classroom is the responsibility of the Christian worker. When the instructor deals with the willfulness and disobedience in a child, others take note of the correction and will be better off. "When the righteous are in authority the people rejoice; but when the wicked beareth rule, the people mourn."[24]

To Build Character

To separate Christian character from Christian living is impossible because, as a child develops, his character is demonstrated through his

life. The child attains good character by controlling his life.
Discipline is something that an adult does for a child, not to a child.
If the adult trains the young people appropriately, he will discover that he
is doing less correcting. Godly discipline will produce character which
will become for the children a way of life. There are two aspects of that
discipline that will assist young people in walking on the right path of life;
according to Beverly LaHaye, those two aspects are preventive discipline
and corrective discipline.[25]

To Encourage Self-Discipline

"Teaching children to develop inner controls over their impulses by
disciplinary practices is clearly one of the most important functions,"[26]
says Charles Schaefer. Children who learn to control their selfish
responses will not only make their surroundings more pleasant, but they
will also be happier. DeZafra writes,

> The ultimate, unique achievement of good discipline is self-discipline
> on the part of the pupils. Experience tells us that not all groups or all
> individuals are likely to become completely self-disciplined with the
> school years, yet that is the goal toward which we must strive. Any
> philosophy of discipline which does not teach and instill the ideal of
> self-discipline within the group and the individual will eventually prove
> weak and ineffective.[27]

In order that they might become disciples of the Lord Jesus Christ,
children need to be shown that they will find joy by leading self-disciplined lives. No one can be a true disciple of Christ, however, until he first
becomes a self-disciplined Christian.

To Enhance Learning

The greatest amount of learning occurs when there is effective control on the part of the instructor who imposes definite behavioral requirements. Such confident discipline assures the teacher that his academic
goals will be achieved through control of the time and of the learners. On
the other hand, the teacher who does not have effective control will
hinder the learning skills of the pupils and impede their achievement and
performance. Self-indulgence on the part of the youngster will be encouraged and self-discipline will be impaired.

CONSISTENCY IN DISCIPLINE

Every young person in the class has varied needs; therefore, the
teacher must recognize each pupil as a separate entity. A good teacher
must not show partiality to one student over another. Although impartiality is extremely difficult because every situation is different, young
people expect the person in charge to be consistent in every judgment.

Consistency Creates Credibility

"When a teacher is inconsistent in discipline, he loses the credibility of the students."[28] Every threat that is not carried out creates the impression that the teacher will never carry through with any threat. The student's behavior is geared to what he believes will or will not happen, not to what the teacher says will happen. Thus, the instructor should be consistent, for his predictability will make the children feel more secure.

Playing Favorites Hinders Consistency

Probably nothing will adversely affect an adult's consistency more than his showing partiality to one child over another. Pupils are quick to notice when the instructor has a teacher's pet. This favoritism may be shown to the attractive, the super intelligent, the athletic, or the popular; but no matter toward whom it is directed, the other pupils in the class resent the preference demonstrated by the teacher.

Moodiness Affects Consistency

Being moody can cause a teacher to base his discipline on changeable ideas and desires instead of an orderly system. Moodiness causes students to become confused as to how they should react to the teacher's erratic behavior, for what is correct conduct one day becomes an infraction another day. "Teachers, being human, are subject to moods like everyone else. But moodiness or no, basic values and behavior standards should remain constant."[29] Therefore, the teacher who knows he has a problem with moodiness needs to allow Christ to give him the victory in that area of his life.

LOVE AND DISCIPLINE

Discipline without love borders on cruelty and is not Biblical. Everything that a servant of God does should be permeated with love; love is the ingredient that makes the difference. Paul tells us that

> Love suffereth long, and is kind; love envieth not; love vaunteth not itself, is not puffed up. Doth not behave itself unseemly, seeketh not her own, is not easily provoked, thinketh no evil; rejoiceth not in iniquity, but rejoiceth in the truth. Beareth all things, believeth all things, hopeth all things, endureth all things. Love never faileth.[30]

Unless the above verses are appropriated into the teacher's life, he will have no influence or consequences.

Love and discipline must stand side by side with the teacher in his day-to-day dealings with the students. Love without discipline is spineless and lacks courage; discipline without love is cold and militaristic. When discipline and love are joined together, the results are an effective tool for guiding, educating, and correcting children.[31] Every youngster needs to know that, although the teacher may not like to discipline him, the teacher stills loves him and always will. As the child realizes that it is his misbehavior that the teacher dislikes and not him, his love and respect will grow deeper, and he will be ashamed of his improper conduct.

GUIDELINES FOR HANDLING DISCIPLINE

Upon entering the classroom of a teacher who is new to them, most young people will be a bit apprehensive as to how the teacher will react to them. A wise teacher will capitalize on that "fear." That teacher will implement a firm, consistent discipline program at the start of school. The pattern of discipline established at the beginning of the school year will tend to be continued throughout the year.

The guidelines that are to follow are only suggestions to correct misbehavior. Since no two situations are exactly alike, these suggestions are not infallible. One technique may be effectively used by one teacher but not by another. Nevertheless, these methods have functioned for many capable instructors and will give assistance to any who are in need of suggestions.

Responding to Minor Infractions

A good teacher will recognize when minor infractions can be "nipped in the bud" before such misbehavior develops into definite punishable offenses. The following suggestions are excellent methods for maintaining general classroom control and keeping minor misbehavior from becoming more serious.

Look at the Student. A look at an offender will often silence him. Gray advises, "Look directly at him while continuing your lecture. Do not pause."[32]

Talk Softer than Usual. "Whisper. Often commands or comments said very softly attract more attention than shouting,"[33] is Rudman's suggestion. Whispering may cause a youngster to cease his distractions in order to listen to the teacher.

Employ Humor. Morse and Wingo advise a teacher to employ humor at times: "Humor may also reduce tension and encourage control."[34] Whereas the teacher must be careful that he does not begin the year by trying to be funny or entertaining, a bit of humor once in a while can be effective in correcting a strained situation.

Use Prearranged Signal. By enacting prearranged signals with the students, the teacher can reduce verbal corrections. These signals might be putting a finger to the lips, turning off the ceiling lights, making a hand motion, and so on.[35]

Capitalize on Body Language. As a general rule, young people will react more quickly to what a teacher does than to what he says. Jones states,

Remember, first and foremost, that you do not train students to
follow rules with your mouth; you train them with your body. Body
language is the all important medium through which you convey
assertiveness, that quality of interaction that tells the child that you
mean business. For the most part, effective teachers say little and
speak softly when setting limits.[36]

The teacher may shake her head, point her finger, or move in a manner that will signal what she desires the students should do.

Be Silent and Stare. According to Ted Christiansen, "Silence is sometimes golden. In most cases, silence is more effective. A 'visual confronta-
tion' often gets the point across and lessens the possibility of public
verbal display."[37]

Ask the Student a Question. Control problems can be reduced when
the Christian worker directs a question about the lesson to the young person distracting the class. A question or even a comment directed to the
offending pupil will cause him to realize that the teacher is aware of his
problem.

Handling Misbehavior that Needs Minor Punishment

Some misbehavior will necessitate some type of overt punishment
for the offender. Greater punishment than those responses listed in the
previous section is demanded, but the offense is not considered to be
sufficiently serious to warrant such action as probation, suspension, or
expulsion.

Call the Pupil's Name. If one of the previous suggestions does not
work, the instructor should call the student's name in a firm tone of voice.

Walk Back to the Student. The next progressive step toward a youngster who does not respond to the previous warnings is to walk back to
where he is sitting.

If he is so engrossed in his misbehavior that he doesn't realize
you have seen him, continue your lecture and walk slowly towards his
seat. As your voice grows louder, he will become conscious of your
approach and glance in your direction.

If he stops before you arrive at his seat, continue on your way to
him anyway. Stand beside him and conduct your class from there for
a minute or so. Let him sweat.[38]

Writing Sentences. If the teacher desires to use writing as a punishment, he should have the youngster copy something neatly from a book
or an encyclopedia. Perchance the child might learn something in the
process; he certainly will not learn anything by writing 500 times, "I will
not talk in class without permission."

Reprimand Verbally. Probably the most commonly used punishment
by a teacher is that of an oral rebuke. This rebuke may be a short, soft-
spoken phrase or a strong, authoritative sentence. Whatever the tone of

the teacher, the student should know that the teacher is directing his correction toward him. The words should not be spoken in anger, but the teacher should measure his words and choose them deliberately for the good of all.

Ask to See Him After Class. When a young person does not respond to some of the previous corrections, the teacher should say in a strong, authoritative voice that he wants to see him after class. If at all possible, the teacher should hold his consultation with the pupil privately so that he might explain why he did not comply with the previous warnings. During this conference the instructor might warn the student that should his behavior not improve, his seat will be moved to the front of the room. Since most pupils do not like to have their seats changed, they will usually shape up. This brief meeting with the student should last for a few brief moments with the teacher giving more of a warning rather than having a long discussion about the young person's behavior.

Change the Young Person's Seat. Because a young person indicates by his conduct that he cannot function quietly where he is sitting, the teacher should move him to the front of the room. After all, he had been warned. He must once again, however, be aware of the reason the teacher has changed his seat.

Deprive the Student of Privileges. Sometimes a teacher can bring about behavior changes by depriving a youngster of certain school privileges:

> Corrective measures that temporarily deny a misbehaving pupil his rights and privileges in a particular situation may be applied if the individual is helped to understand the relationship between the denials and his uncooperative behavior.[39]

Embarrass the Student. This was a tactic that was used occasionally by the Lord Jesus. Most of the time a teacher should endeavor to settle a problem in privacy; however, an incident might arise when the teacher may have to embarrass a student if he feels that such a maneuver would be best for everyone concerned. Precaution should be used in this area.

Isolate from Other Students. "If breaches of good conduct continue," comments de Zafra, "move the pupil to an isolated seat in the rear of the room until he is ready to be 'readmitted' to the class."[40] The youngster can be isolated from opportunities of participating in activities and special privileges until his problem is settled. This isolation could be within the classroom, on the playground, or in the dining hall; but wherever the youngster is isolated, he must be supervised by some adult. Never is the child to be left by himself, nor should his separation be extended over a long period of time.

Dealing with Offenses That Need More Severe Punishment

A teacher needs to have a plan for dealing with more serious offenses and minor offenses that have not been stopped through less severe punishment. The school's discipline system may specify the teacher's response to such misbehavior.

Hold a Teacher-Student Conference. Kindsuatter believes that "the most effective control technique for serious misbehavior is the private teacher-student conference."[41] Such a meeting can enable the teacher to reinforce his position on the standards and to gain insight into unknown problems concerning the pupil. Also, in these personal conferences, the Christian worker should learn to listen and to ask the kind of questions that will elicit information pertinent to the student's problem.

Communicate with Parents by Note or Phone Call. By warning the pupil that he will send a note or phone call to his parents, the teacher may help the young person decide to straighten out. But he will have to send the note or call the parents if the student does not correct his deviate conduct. Most parents will appreciate being informed of their child's problem so that they may give support to the teacher.

Send the Student to Another Classroom. Arrangements might be made with another teacher to send the problem child to his room. The class to which the youngster is sent should be a well-run classroom with a strong disciplinarian in charge. During the time the pupil is in the other room, he should have to sit quietly in the back of the class and do assigned work. This technique is always more effective if the youngster is put in a room three or four grades below his level because he will not want his classmates to see him in the company of younger children.

Assign the Student to Detention. Students are kept after school for a minimum of forty-five minutes under strict rules of conduct and study. If proper discipline is not maintained, all efforts to correct behavior are lost. Parents should be notified a day in advance, so that they might make arrangements for their children's transportation from school.

Lower the Conduct Mark. Giving a low conduct mark is a type of punishment. Many young people may not be personally concerned with their conduct grade; but their parents probably will care and, as a result, will bring pressure on their offspring.

Arrange a Supervisor-Student Conference. For the sake of everyone concerned, the teacher should let the supervisor know of a continual problem with any child. Because the supervisor is usually more experienced in dealing with students, he may be able to handle the difficulty using a different approach. However, if the supervisor is unsuccessful in correcting the student's attitudes, he may have to resort to phoning the student's parents to arrange a conference with them.

Send the Child to the Principal. A problem student should be sent to the principal only as a last resort. Certainly, if the teacher cannot straighten out the child, by all means he should send him to the office without any apologies or defensive explanations.

Hold a Teacher-Parent Conference. Eventually, the teacher may have to request a meeting with at least one of the parents. At this meeting it would be advisable for the teacher to have a record of the different problems with the youngster and of how those problems were handled. The parent should see how the instructor progressively dealt with each situation. Most of the time a parent will express his appreciation for the teacher's concern and will assure his cooperation to correct the trouble.

Send a Letter from the Principal. Before taking the final step, the principal should send a letter to the parents stating what the problems have been and the consequences should the pupil not comply with the standards of the school. In this letter the parents should be invited to consult with the principal for a conference with him and the teacher involved.

Place the Student on Conduct Probation. Still another type of punishment is placing the student on probation because of improper behavior over a long period of time. The probation period should be no shorter than two weeks and no longer than six. If the young person has a desire to participate in an activity or to stay in the school, he will feel the pressure of this punishment and will attempt to alter his ways.

Administer Corporal Punishment. There are diverse approaches to corporal punishment in Christian schools; there are also various regulations required of the teachers when they think that paddling is necessary. The teacher must follow the policy of the school in this area. Whoever administers the paddling must be calm and patient and should have an adult as a witness. It is advisable that parents be notified before punishment is administered.

Use Suspension or Expulsion as Last Resort. Stevens says, "Finally. . . it may be necessary to suspend or to expel a student if behavior becomes detrimental to other students or to the functioning of the school program."[42] If the punishment is to be suspension, the student should not spend the day at home watching television. He should instead have an At-School Suspension in which he is isolated from his classmates while he works on assignments that have been given to him by his teachers. A suspension should not be a fun time spent at home.

There may be a time when the administration will have to expel a student because he and his parents will not cooperate with the school. After trying the aforementioned ways of dealing with the pupil, the teacher and the administration should not feel guilty for having to deal with the young person in such a manner. Even the Lord Jesus Christ had a follower who would not respond to Him. Wilson points out that

Judas Iscariot was the one disciple whom Jesus let go. He had wonderful opportunities to be influenced by the Master Teacher, but he did not take proper advantage of them. Like the other disciples, he came as an ordinary man with an ordinary nature, but unlike the others he came to a point where he rejected the teachings of Jesus.

In the experience of teachers (and principals) today, there are "heart-break" pupils who simply will not be won, and ultimately have to be given up. If this was Jesus' experience with Judas Iscariot, it is possible that all other teachers or principals might have to face such a situation.[43]

DO'S AND DON'TS FOR MAINTAINING DISCIPLINE

Many teachers have said that they need assistance in managing their classes. The following Do's and Don'ts are some fundamental principles which will improve not only classroom control, but also pupil response and interest.

The Teacher Should ...

Ask for God's Wisdom — James 1:5: "If any of you lack wisdom, let him ask of God . . ." The Lord desires to supply wisdom, but the teacher must ask for it.

Exemplify Self-discipline — When a teacher does not demonstrate self-control in and out of the classroom, he loses his credibility.

Establish Standards — From the very beginning the teacher should define the limitations for the pupils. It is more desirable to be strict at the start, then loosen up as the school year progresses. The instructor will find it easier to let up on control than to tighten up after control has been lost.

Avoid Perfectionism — No teacher is perfect, nor should he expect his students to be.

Establish Routines — From the beginning, the teacher should establish routines. Young people will know what to expect, and thus there will be less confusion.

Hear a Child Out — Many times a youngster wants to be able to tell why he did what he did. This does not mean that the teacher will accept his explanation, but at least the child has had the opportunity to explain his actions.

Develop Awareness — Some teachers are completely oblivious to motion and distractions. The person in charge should keep in mind that he has the responsibility of aiding the young people to manage themselves.

Deal with a Problem as Soon as Possible — "Because sentence against an evil work is not executed speedily, therefore the heart of the sons of men is fully set in them to do evil" (Ecclesiastes 8:11). Shaheen declares, "Punishment should be swift, reasonable, related to the offense, and absolutely certain to occur — it does not have to be severe."[44]

Admit When Wrong — It is imperative that a teacher admit when he is wrong. When an instructor acknowledges a mistake, his students have a deeper respect for him, and they will learn to admit when they make mistakes.

Have Students Raise Hands and Wait To Be Called On — This procedure will eliminate many problems. When pupils blurt out questions and answers, it is distracting for everyone.

Respond to the Child — Ignoring a pupil will cause him to feel rejected, for even a reprimand on the part of the teacher shows him that the teacher cares.

Demand Respect — The Christian worker should remember that he is training the child for life; therefore, the teacher should insist that respect be shown to him and to all adults.

Try to Anticipate a Problem — A teacher should think things through, foresee possible pitfalls, and get them cleared up before they become a problem.

Try to Handle His Own Problems — By handling his own discipline, the teacher will create confidence in himself and gain respect from the students. The students will lose confidence in the teacher who is constantly seeking help from a higher authority.

Praise Pupils for Good Behavior — The most effective method of control has been that of commending pupils for proper behavior, for students will strive for attention and praise from a teacher whom they respect and admire.

Pray for Discipline Problems — God desires to change improper behavior, especially that which is willful and rebellious. Through love and prayer, desired conduct can be achieved.

The Teacher Should . . .

Never Condone Improper Behavior — The teacher might think that siding with the guilty party will win his friendship, but in reality the teacher's condoning improper behavior will result in his losing the respect of the other pupils.

Never Accuse without Proof — By objectively gathering relevant facts, the teacher will have definite proof before administering any penalties.

Never Punish the Group for Offenses of a Few — It is not right to castigate the innocent with the guilty few. Such unfair action will only develop resentment from those who are not guilty.[45] "Also to punish the just is not good" (Prov. 17:26).

Never Use Sarcasm or Ridicule — Making a sarcastic remark or ridiculing a pupil will antagonize students against the teacher, and he will eventually have the group against him.

Never Make a Threat He Cannot Carry Out — If the teacher makes threats with little action behind them, after awhile they will mean very little to the students. Meaningless warnings are of no value to anyone.

Never Punish When Angry — No student should ever be punished because he is offensive to the teacher, because the teacher loses his patience, because he is not liked, or because the teacher wants to get back at him. No punishment should ever be given unless the main motive is correction through love.

Never Play Favorites — Naturally some pupils are more appealing to a teacher than others because of their friendliness or abilities, but no one should receive any special privileges because of those attributes.

Never Tolerate "High Looks" or "Making Faces" — These are rebellious facial gestures that indicate the child is in open disagreement with the teacher. "A high look and a proud heart . . . is sin" (Proverbs 21:4).

Never Record a "D" or "F" Without Notifying Parent First — The parent should have been previously notified in some way.

Never Give Special Privileges to Discipline Problems — Privileges should be an honor and must be earned. If a child constantly misbehaves and is then given benefits like everyone else, he is being rewarded for his misbehavior.

Never Withdraw Affection from a Misbehaving Youngster — The teacher may not be pleased with the actions of the child, but that does not mean that he should dislike the child. No matter what the pupil does, the teacher should still love him in Christ. A child can sense the true feelings of an adult.

Never Call a Child "Dumb" or "Stupid" — Such statements can create an attitude of defeat in a child. There are probably no other words that will crush a young person's spirit like these two words; therefore, they have no place in the vocabulary of a teacher when he is correcting.

Never Commit the Administration — The teacher should never commit the administration to a punishment. For instance, the teacher should not say, "If you do that one more time, I am going to take you to the principal, and he is going to expel you from school." Maybe the principal will not think the offense merits such harsh punishment, and therefore, the teacher would be embarrassed because his threat is not carried out.

Never Say "Shut Up!" — This is a very crude expression and has no place in the classroom.

Never Lower Grade for Improper Conduct — It does injustice to both academic grades and conduct grades when they are mixed; keep them separate.

Never Depend on Paddling to Maintain Control — It should be the desire of every Christian school to use corporal punishment as little, but as effectively, as possible.

Never Cast Reflections on a Child's Family — A child cannot help what his father or mother is like, nor can he help being poor; therefore in punishing a child, a teacher should never speak disrespectfully of a youngster's parents.

Never Snap Fingers or Say "Sh-h-h" — These are both meaningless and ineffective sounds. Instead of these sounds the teacher should use words with significance.

Never Exhaust All Disciplinary Resources — The teacher should say and do as little as possible and still get results. If some disciplinary resources are kept in reserve, the teacher will have some actions to fall back on.

Never Allow Improper Behavior to Succeed — If, after punishment has been administered, it has not proven effective, a negative outcome will result. For instance, a teacher takes a young person outside the room to warn him concerning his conduct. If, after the talk with the teacher in the hall, the student reenters the room with a broad, defiant grin on his face, the second state is worse than the first.[45]

CONCLUSION

The Christian should control his class from the very first day, but he must realize that because discipline is a process, it takes time. Because young people come from various backgrounds and have different needs, the teacher must have patience, steadfastness, and, above all, love. Children will make mistakes simply because they are children. If they did not require correction and guidance, there would be no necessity for them to be under the tutelage of adults; however, children are not adults and should not be expected to behave as such.

> The child learns from his mistakes as well as from his successes, especially if the mistakes are evaluated and the corrections are indicated. No real harm can come from a mistake if the pupil recognizes that it is a mistake. In other words, he should learn to make victory out of defeat.[47]

Then, too, the young person will be more easily guided when there is a positive relationship between him and the teacher. Very often the two can achieve this positive relationship when the adult accepts the youngster as an important creation of God. His acceptance should be demonstrated through encouragement, friendliness, and genuine concern. If the child does not feel accepted, any correction, no matter how well intended, will have an improper effect. When, however, there is a proper relationship, the pupil will not want to disappoint the teacher whom he respects. In other words, the child will want to be like the teacher, and he will care about what the adult thinks of his behavior.[48]

When the Christian teacher applies the principles of discipline found in the Bible, not only will he be a blessing for the Lord, but he will be a strength to the children. Without the guidance of the Holy Spirit, the teacher's efforts are merely the work of the flesh and will accomplish little here on earth and less for eternity. After all, teaching with eternity in mind is what a Christian school is all about.

FOOTNOTES

[1]Richard Kindsuatter, "A New View of the Dynamics of Discipline," *Phi Delta Kappan,* January 1978, p. 322.

[2]Carlos deZafra, Jr., *62 Suggestions to Improve Classroom Discipline* (Fairfield, N.J.: The Economics Press, Inc., 1968), p. 1.

[3]Frederic H. Jones, "The Gentle Art of Classroom Discipline," *Elementary School Principals Journal,* July 1979, pp. 26-27.

[4]James Dobson, *Dare to Discipline* (Wheaton, Ill.: Tyndale House Pub., 1973), p. 109.

[5]H.W. Byrne, *A Christian Approach to Education* (Milford, Michigan: Mott Media, 1977), p. 130.

[6]Thomas Good and Jere Brophy, *Looking in Classrooms* (New York: Harper and Row Pub., 1973), p. 93.

[7]Thelma Johnson, "Kindergarten Discipline and Habits," *Philosophy of Discipline Syllabus* (Pensacola, Fl.: A Beka Book Pub., 1979), p. 7.

[8]Ibid., pp. 6-7.

[9]Thomas Smith, "The Christian Philosophy of Discipline," *The Christian Educator,* January 1976, p. 6.

[10]Robert L. Schain and Murray Polner, *Using Effective Discipline for Better Class Control* (New York: Teachers Practical Press, Inc., 1966), p. 48.

[11]Marsha Rudman, "Discipline," *Instructor,* August/September 1976, p. 67.

[12]Walter E. McPhie, "Discipline Problems: An Educational Malignancy," *National Association of Secondary School Principals,* December 1961, p. 82.

[13]Emma Edmunds and Gayle White, "Principal Is Key to Orderly School," *The Atlanta Constitution,* June 9, 1978, Sec. 8, p. 1.

[14]Barbara Bradley, "Elementary Discipline," *Philosophy of Discipline Syllabus* (Pensacola, Fla.: A Beka Book Pub., 1979), p. 17.

[15]Muriel Schoenbrun Karlin and Regina Berger, *Discipline and the Disruptive Child* (West Nyack, NY: Parker Pub., Co., Inc., 1972), p. 20.

[16]DeZafra, Jr., p. 1.

[17]Jones, p. 27.

[18]James Dobson, *Hide or Seek* (Wheaton, Ill.: Fleming H. Revell Co., 1971), p. 156.

[19]Dobson, *Dare to Discipline,* p. 125.

[20]Ibid.

[21]Thomas L. Smith, *What Every Parent Should Know about Christian Education* (Murfreesboro: The Christian Educator Pub., 1976), p. 50.

[22]Charles E. Schaefer, "Practice Exchange on Punishment," *Child Care Quarterly,* 5 (Winter 1976), 312.

[23]Proverbs 21:11.

[24]Proverbs 29:2.

[25]Beverly LaHaye, *How to Develop Your Child's Temperament* (Irvine: Harvest House Pub., 1977), pp. 142-143.

[26]Schaefer, p. 307.

[27]DeZafra, Jr., p. 2.

[28]Good and Brophy, p. 169.

[29]William C. Morse and G. Max Wingo, *Psychology and Teaching,* 3rd ed. (Atlanta: Scott, Foresman Co., 1969), p. 323.

[30]I Corinthians 13:4-8.

[31]LaHaye, p. 140.

[32]Jenny Gray, *The Teacher's Survival Guide* (Palo Alto, California: Fearon Pub., 1967), p. 22.

[33]Rudman, p. 87.

[34]Morse and Wingo, p. 429.

[35]Rudman, p. 87.

[36]Jones, p. 29.

[37]Ted Christiansen, "10 Commandments of Classroom Discipline," *New Mexico School Review,* Vol. 48, p. 1.

[38]Gray, p. 23.

[39]Lester D. Crow and Alice Crow, *The Student Teacher in the Elementary School* (New York: David McKay Co., Inc., 1965), p. 338.

[40]DeZafra, Jr., p. 27.

[41]Kindsuatter, p. 325.

[42]Andrew Stevens, "Techniques for Handling Problem Parents," *Handbook of Successful School Administration* (Englewood Cliffs, New Jersey: Prentice-Hall, Inc., 1976), p. 645.

[43]Clifford A. Wilson, *Jesus the Teacher* (Melbourne, Australia: Word of Truth Productions Lt., 1974), pp. 85-86.

[44]JoAnn Shaheen, "Guidelines for Discipline," quoted by Eugene R. Howard, *School Discipline Desk Book* (West Nyack, N.Y.: Parker Pub. Co., Inc., 1978), p. 97.

[45]DeZafra, Jr., p. 18.

[46]Dobson, *Dare to Discipline*, p. 88.

[47]Blanche McDonald and Leslie Nelson, *Successful Classroom Control* (Dubuque, Iowa: Wm. C. Brown Co., 1955), p. 71.

[48]Schaefer, pp. 308-309.

QUESTIONS AND PROBLEMS

1. When thinking of a classroom, why is the word "control" better than the word "discipline"?

2. Why do you think many colleges do not train prospective teachers in the area of classroom control?

3. Can you remember a teacher in elementary or high school who could not control his/her class? What was your attitude toward that teacher then? What do you think of that teacher now?

4. In thinking back over your experiences in elementary and high school, what irritated you the most concerning teachers and their discipline?

5. Name other things not mentioned in this chapter that you think a teacher should or should not do as far as their pupils are concerned.

6. Can you think of reasons why some teachers compromise their standards with students in order to be accepted and liked?

7. Do you agree with the opening paragraph in this chapter?

8. Did you ever have a teacher in school that you thought was too strict? Explain.

Classroom
Procedures

Chapter 6

VI
CLASSROOM PROCEDURES

"Routinization of procedures justifies itself in that both time and effort are conserved when an action of necessity performed daily is habituated," says Brown.[1] Recent research on teacher effectiveness suggests that those who show the most gains in achievements in the classroom are those who rely on traditional management methods of instruction, at least in basic skills. The reason for this is that time and effort are not wasted because procedures have been established.[2] The importance of saving time should be evident in all procedures in order for them to become habitual.

Because routines become a matter of building customs into the pupils in the classroom, they ultimately eliminate waste of time and effort. The routines must be established at the beginning of the school year, then drilled upon and held to rigidly until all tendencies to act in any other way have been entirely overcome.[3] It does not take pupils long to learn that in school things go better with order, and order will enable the teacher and student to work more efficiently with one another. Mursell believes that:

> Such matters as seating, taking attendance, dismissing the class, the passing and returning of papers, etc., should be planned and routinized with care, for they are all opportunities on the one hand for teaching proper concerted action, or on the other for disorder and the generation of bad attitudes.[4]

GENERAL PROCEDURES FOR THE TEACHER

Every aspect of the classroom will be more enjoyable and efficient when the teacher and the pupils work together through organization. Organizing routines are called procedures. The more effectively those procedures are carried out, the more productive will be the work in the classroom. The following are some suggestions for making the classroom more enjoyable and efficient.

The Classroom Itself

It is the teacher's responsibility to make his classroom attractive for the enjoyment of the children. Colorful pictures, wall displays, original decorations, and attractive plants will all combine to make a joyful experience for the young people who occupy it. Not only will a cheerful room do wonders for the morale of the students, but it will keep the spirit of the teacher in a more happy frame of mind. Says Gray, even "Bulletin boards can be superb visual aids for teaching a unit, setting a mood, or getting across a point."[5] Other aspects of the room decor should incorporate learning elements.

The environment of the classroom should not only contain elements for learning but should be physically comfortable as well. Consequently, the teacher must be constantly sensitive to lighting, room temperature, and ventilation. In addition to these things, keeping the room neat is the responsibility of the teacher. "Books, periodicals, desks, chairs should be kept in orderly array," suggests Drayer. "A half-erased chalkboard can make an otherwise neat room appear sloppy."[6]

Punctuality

By all means, in order to demonstrate to the young people that punctuality is important, the teacher should be in the classroom when the students arrive. Being an early bird will help the teacher bring about a calm start; otherwise, he may have a hard time controlling the students due to his own lack of punctuality.[7] Students who are welcomed to school by a locked room are not receiving the welcome they deserve, declares Weaver. "Futhermore," he continues, "they are learning that promptness is not important."[8]

The Seating Chart

The administration will probably give the teacher some sort of class roster before the first day. If at all possible, the instructor should practice the pronunciation of students' names ahead of time. The school does expect the roll to be checked and an accurate record of absences and tardies turned in every day. If the teacher makes a seating chart beforehand, he will be able to take the roll more easily. "No educational benefit is realized when students listen to their classmates saying 'here.' " Jenny Gray continues, " It is very boring and classroom buzz takes over in no time at all."[9]

In addition to aiding in taking the roll, a seating chart will enable a substitute teacher to know the names of the students more readily. Still another point regarding the seating chart is that the names should be written in pencil, because undoubtedly someone will have to have his or her seat changed before the school year is out, and names written in pencil are easier to erase.

Regarding the seating of young people, the row formation has been found to be much more conducive to better control. With the introduction of the "open" classroom concept, some teachers thought that the clustering of children together in table formations brought about scholastic behavior. However, observations of pupils who sat at tables showed that they were more disruptive in their behavior than those children who sat in rows.[10]

The Gradebook and Class Records

Sloppy records and messy gradebooks are a poor testimony for Christian teachers who are told in the Bible that everything should "be done decently and in order."[11] With an accurate record of absences and a correct recording of assignments, the teacher can determine exactly what the students must do for make-up work. The gradebook should also reflect the accomplishments and shortcomings of the pupils in their class work. In addition to these things, the teacher should keep a record of the times that parents have been contacted concerning problems and honors.

The Beginning of School

One of the most important aspects of education is getting off to a good start, according to Drayer. "When meeting a class for the first time," he says, "the teacher should explain his procedures, standards, and regulations, and reasons for them."[12] As a general rule, it is better for the teacher to be somewhat strict at the beginning rather than too lenient; later, if he wants to, he can relax a bit as the young people adjust to his authority. However, after the teacher has set standards and procedures, he must make sure the students hold to his regulations.

Starting the Class with Prayer

One of the distinct differences between Christian schools and non-Christian is that in a Christian school every class can and should begin with prayer. When the teacher asks the students to pray with him, he is indicating to them that he needs God's help in the classroom. Such prayers should be an encouragement to young people to seek the Lord to assist them as they go throughout life.

Giving Directions

Another aspect of good classroom procedures is giving clear directions that cut down on confusion and misunderstanding. Effective directions can save the teacher a great deal of time and effort, since he will not have to keep repeating and clarifying what he has already said. Sidney and Iris Tiedt offer the following suggestions for giving directions:

1. Be sure **you** understand the process being described.
2. Do not begin speaking until everyone is listening.
3. Speak clearly and loudly enough so all can hear.
4. Use understandable language that is familiar to the students. Explain any unknown terms.
5. Tell the children the object of the lesson.
6. Don't try to cover too much with one set of directions. If the project is complicated, work in stages. You may wish to duplicate instructions so that each student will have a guide or outline to follow.
7. Have children repeat the directions. Ask them questions to see if they understand.[13]

Neatness of Written Work

A teacher's efficiency can often be measured by the character of the papers turned in to him by his students. Sloppy writing, ugly erasure marks, smudges on the paper, words written over, or indeed papers torn from notebooks and even wrinkled — such carelessness should not be tolerated by the teacher who wants young people to do their best for Christ. These things may not seem important to some teachers, but they play a significant role in the training of proper habits. The instructor needs to be exact in what he expects as far as form and neatness are concerned, and then he should keep insisting on his standards until they become routine. According to Bagley, "The ability to train pupils to produce accurate written work is a fairly good index of the teacher's general capacity in habit-building."[14]

Class Participation

A teacher should establish definite rules governing the procedures for class discussions and other forms of class participation. These rules should be rigidly enforced until everyone conforms to them automatically. It is hoped that the students will learn that the etiquette of classroom courtesy will not cramp them but will actually free them to communicate better.[15]

Recitation is perhaps the most often used method of teaching. When using such, Blaney suggests that the teacher respond to a child's performance. By responding, the teacher will give a reinforcement whether it be positive or otherwise. If the pupil has contributed something worthwhile, however, he should compliment the student's participation.[16]

In class discussions, the Christian worker must control two extremes that may exist in the class. He must encourage the timid students by directing questions along the line of their interests or by asking them to give their opinions on a certain topic. After they give such responses, the teacher must express appreciation for their contributions so that they will feel confident and want to reply again. On the other hand, the teacher must keep those who think they know more than the teacher from monopolizing the time. These students are not to be ignored, but they must be held in check in order for others to have opportunities to share their thoughts and ideas. It is the teacher's responsibility to keep the discussion moving toward the goals that he has set; otherwise, the lesson will drag and important results will be lost.[17]

Routine Matters

There is evidence that classroom organization and management skills are closely related to instructional skills; consequently, good instructors tend to be good managers.[18] A teacher who is a good manager establishes certain routines in order to conserve time and to develop security on the part of the pupils who need to know what to expect in a given situation. Some procedures are the following: 1) checking attendance, 2) distributing pupil's written work, 3) checking homework, 4) dispensing learning materials, 5) practicing fire drills, 6) keeping the room clean, 7) moving about the classroom, 8) returning books and equipment to shelves, 9) emptying the wastebaskets, 10) entering and leaving the room, 11) keeping desks and tables neat and clean, 12) hanging up wraps, and 13) storing lunch boxes.[19]

OTHER PROCEDURES FOR THE CLASSROOM

"Successful classroom managers spend a great deal of time early in the year conducting semi-formal lessons to familiarize students with rules and procedures,"[20] says Brophy. Of course, a teacher should not begin the school year with a long list of regulations, but as a problem arises, he may want to establish a procedure concerning any one of the following:

The Teacher's Desk

From the start of school, the teacher should not allow students to become familiar with his desk. He should never permit them to sit in his chair nor to handle personal objects on his desk. And certainly, pupils should never open the drawers of his desk without special permission.

Assigning Work at the Board

Since there is never space for all members of the class at the board at one time, procedures must be established to avoid confusion and loss of time. The teacher could assign work by rows, for one thing, but he should never have all of the assigned students at the board at one time. Taller young people should be given space at the top of the board while shorter folks might work at levels they can reach.

Dealing with Forgetfulness

By establishing sound habits of preparedness, the teacher will reinforce the behavior of those who try to remember to have their materials in place at the right time. The student should know that if he is not prepared, he will have to suffer the consequences of being forgetful or careless. Never should a teacher allow young people to borrow forgotten materials from one another because such a practice only adds to irresponsibility.

Passing Notes in Class

"Good teaching allows little time for note writing."[21] There should be an understanding early in the school year that passing notes will not be tolerated. The teacher might even give a warning that any note that is intercepted will be read aloud to the class; however, precautions must be taken for notes that are improper.

Poor Posture

A youngster may develop an unhealthy posture if not corrected, and improper posture can lead to poor penmanship and messy papers.[22] Therefore, it is the teacher's responsibility to remind young people that they are to sit up in their desks.

Tidiness around Pupils' Desks

Brown and Phelps believe that "Pupils as well as teachers are inclined to be messy in their housekeeping."[23] Periodically the teacher may have to remind the students to straighten up their belongings under their desks so that tidiness is maintained in the classroom. A good motto is, "A place for everything, and everything in its place."

Eating during Classes

School rules usually do not permit young people to eat while the class is in progress because pupils cannot concentrate on their studies and food at the same time. Therefore, the teacher needs to enforce the rule of not eating during class.

Chewing Gum in Classes

Along the same line as eating in class is chewing gum. Chewing gum, in itself, of course, is no sin; but it can become such a maintenance problem that most schools have restrictions against it.

Bathroom Breaks

Collins and Collins discuss bathroom breaks in a rather humorous way. "The bathroom," they say, "holds a special fascination for students of all ages. For the student who is bored, unsure of himself, or just 'seat-sick,' it is a plausible retreat."[24] There are times when young people have legitimate reasons to use the bathroom, and the teacher will probably be able to recognize those instances. He will, however, have to make sure that those privileges are not abused.

Pencil Sharpening

Pupils should realize that they are not allowed to go to the pencil sharpener whenever they desire because this will be too distracting to the rest of the class. A specific time should be designated by the teacher for the young people to take care of writing utensils; otherwise, there will probably be a constant stream of pupils sharpening their pencils.

Doodling

"Doodling in the classroom is an irritant to some teachers who feel that only direct attention to them manifests guaranteed thinking."[25] Some young people doodle on workbooks by drawing ugly and grotesque things. Because those workbooks are used in the classroom, the teacher has every right to prohibit students from producing such eyesores in his room. It is hoped that the students will learn to take better care of their property if the teacher insists on their doing so.

Head on Desk

A teacher should not tolerate nap-taking in his class, nor should he allow a young person even to put his head on the desk. If a youngster has his head on his desk because he does not feel well, the teacher should send him to the office; but if he says he is not sick, then he should be told to keep his head off the desk. Gray tells those who take naps in class, "Sleep on your own time, not mine."[26]

Dismissal of the Class

Since dismissing a class early can be a problem for other classes that are still in session, it is advisable for the teacher to keep his students in class until the bell rings to signal the end of the period. The teacher dismisses the class; the bell does not dismiss them. Of course, it is also true that the person in charge should not retain the young people in his class after the bell has rung; otherwise, they will be late to the next class.

CONCLUSION

The school is an institution in which young people associate with others of comparable ages and learn to grow and to develop in order to become productive individuals. Classroom organization either promotes or hinders the development of correct behavior. It is possible to organize in such a way that practically all reasons for personal clashes will be eliminated. Habits which develop from good room organization, and which are basically habits of social relationships include the following:

Punctuality: keeping appointments; obeying promptly; performing tasks promptly; returning borrowed articles promptly; arriving at school on time; turning in written work on time; retiring and getting up at regular hours; promptness in acknowledging kindnesses.

Obedience: obeying willingly and cheerfully; obeying intelligently, without thought of reward, without being watched, and without reservation; obeying constituted authority; obeying the rules laid down for a good citizen; obeying without asking why?

Social Honesty: returning borrowed property promptly; maintaining fairness (not cheating) in examinations; respecting the property of others; keeping promises; avoiding exaggeration; sticking to what the child believes is right in the face of opposition.

Courtesy: awaiting his turn; refraining from loud talking and laughing which distrubs others; refraining from interrupting others; performing small services for others such as holding open the door, picking up dropped articles, and offering his chair.

Cooperation: working and playing with others; working for the good of all; helping to keep the room, building, and grounds clean; doing one's share in assembly programs; aiding cheerfully in all kinds of school undertakings; doing a job well, even a job one dislikes; accepting responsibility; working hard on all cooperative enterprises.[27]

Efficient classroom procedures will help the students develop habits that will enable both them and the teacher to function more efficiently and happily in an environment conducive to learning.

FOOTNOTES

[1]Edwin John Brown, *Managing the Classroom* (New York: The Ronald Press Company, 1952), p. 182.

[2]Robert L. Blaney, "Effective Teaching in Early Childhood Education," *The Elementary School Journal,* 80 (January 1980), p. 128.

[3]William Chandler Bagley, *Classroom Management* (New York: The Macmillan Company, 1911), p. 17.

[4]James L. Mursell, *The Psychology of Secondary School* (New York: W.W. Norton and Company, Inc., 1932), pp. 460-461.

[5]Jenny Gray, *The Teacher's Survival Guide* (Palo Alto, California: Fearon Publishers, 1967), p. 16.

[6]Adam M. Drayer, *Problems and Methods in High School Teaching* (Boston: D.C. Heath and Company, 1963), p. 216.

[7]S. Gray Garwood, "Ten Ways to Prevent Classroom Chaos," *Instructor,* October 1976, p. 75.

[8]Galen R. Weaver, "The Teacher Being An Example of Self-Discipline," *Chronicle of Christian Education* (Bangor Maine: Maine Association of Christian Schools, October 1981), p. 4.

[9]Gray, p. 38.

[10]Sal Axelrod, R. Vance Hall, and Ann Tams, "Comparison of Two Common Classroom Seating Arrangements," *Academic Therapy,* 15 (September 1979), 35.

[11]I Corinthians 14:40.

[12]Drayer, p. 4.

[13]Sidney W. Tiedt and Iris M. Tiedt, *The Elementary Teacher's Complete Handbook* (Englewood Cliffs, New Jersey: Prentice-Hall, Inc., 1965), p. 7.

[14]Bagley, p. 47.

[15]Nelson L. Bossing, *Teaching in Secondary Schools,* 3rd ed. (Boston: Houghton Mifflin Company, 1952), p. 452.

[16]Blaney, p. 129.

[17]Herbert H. Mills and Harl R. Douglas, *Teaching in High School,* 2nd ed. (New York: The Ronald Press Co., 1957), p. 195.

[18]Jere E. Brophy, "Advances in Teacher Research," *The Journal of Classroom Interaction,* 15 (Winter 1979), 3.

[19]Marie A. Mehl, Hubert H. Mills, and Harl R. Douglas, *Teaching in Elementary School* (New York: The Ronald Press Company, 1958), p. 291.

[20]Brophy, p. 3.

[21]Myrtle Collins and Dwane R. Collins, *Survival Kit for Teachers (and Parents)* (Pacific Palesades, Calif.: The Goodyear Publishing Co., 1975), p. 79.

[22]R.M. Vogelheim, "Effect of Social Reinforcement on Poor Posture," cited in *Therapies for School Behavior Problems* (San Francisco: Jossey-Bass Publishers, 1980), p. 192.

[23]Edwin John Brown and Arthur Thomas Phelps, *Managing the Classroom,* 2nd ed. (New York: The Ronald Press Co., 1961), p. 36.

[24]Collins and Collins, p. 32.

[25]Ibid., p. 64.

[26]Gray, p. 20.

[27]Brown, pp. 185-186.

QUESTIONS AND PROBLEMS

1. How is character taught through classroom procedures?
2. Why is starting the school year with proper classroom procedures so important to effective classroom management?
3. Give precautions concerning classroom prayer time. Suggest various ways of conducting prayer.
4. Sometimes, without even trying, pupils will respond with "I don't know" when asked a question. What should the teacher do to get such students to think through problems and to come up with some kind of an answer?
5. Should teachers or school officials go through the desks, books, and/or lockers of students without asking their permission? Explain.
6. What would you say are your most effective classroom procedures? What are some weak areas in which you could improve?
7. Do you think students pay much attention to the neatness of a classroom? Give reasons to support your answer.
8. Do classroom procedures stifle pupils' personalities? Explain.

Homework

Chapter 7

VII
HOMEWORK

Something new enters the life of the parent of a fourth-grader and continues throughout the rest of the child's school career — homework. Those first assignments may be easy and the child is often very excited by them, but as he goes up the educational ladder, they increase in difficulty and so does his resentment.[1]

Because some students resent homework, there have been many educators and some parents who seriously questioned the worth of work outside of the classroom. They contended that homework was altogether useless and had little value.[2] Other educators considered homework unnecessary and even perhaps harmful. They reasoned that students should be allowed to plan their study programs at their own discretion. But H.G. Rickover believes that that is expecting too much from young people who will elect the easiest and not always the wisest alternative.[3] Regardless of what many liberal educators of the last two decades think about homework, it has become an effective element in the program of the Christian school movement.

TWO CATEGORIES OF HOMEWORK

Whalen writes that whether the homework is given as a particular daily assignment or as a series of long-range assignments, homework can be broken down into two categories. First, there are the assignments that complement the daily instructional program. These assignments are given to complete the lesson that has been presented during the regular class period. Secondly, assignments are sometimes given to expand and/or enrich the subject matter.[4] Such work includes projects and other long-range work.

Naturally, however, the bulk of what a youngster learns will be accomplished in the classroom through lectures, discussions, drills, quizzes, audio-visuals, and other teaching devices. The teacher should never expect the studying outside of the classroom to accomplish what should be achieved during the regular class time.

Tyler believes that the homework process actually involves a sequence of learning experiences in which the student becomes involved in "the learning situation, seeks to practice the things he is to learn, obtains guidance as needed in making his efforts successful, gains satisfaction from successful performances, and continues the practice."[5] These homework experiences are all a part of the learning process that encourages and prods young people to surpass their own previous efforts to attain greater distinctions.[6]

THE PURPOSE OF HOMEWORK

The basic aim of formal education is to prepare the young person to cope with problems once he becomes an adult, and the Christian school uses the Word of God as a guide and force to enable him to achieve this aim. One of the purposes of homework is to encourage the student to exercise his own initiative and self-discipline.

Another purpose is to help the pupil to see the relationship between the facts learned in the classroom and their applications to everyday living. Classroom learning should be reinforced, so that the young person can test his learning achievements for himself through practical experiences.

Still another purpose of homework is to help parents stay abreast of the child's progress.

Hoover contends that homework should establish habits of work. Students who do not develop the habit of achievement after school hours tend to follow the same pattern in their adult lives.[7]

PRINCIPLES RELATED TO THE EFFECTIVE USE OF HOMEWORK

Sterling Callahan suggests the following principles to help the teacher use homework as a learning device:

1. Homework is valuable only if it improves the learning ability of the young people involved. Giving homework just for "busy work" will not accomplish anything but resentment.

2. Homework should be considered a supplement to the work of the classroom lesson. When students see that the material will assist them in their learning process, they are apt to have a better attitude toward it.

3. Students can study well only when their environment is conducive for studying. Some students must be encouraged to seek and develop better conditions for learning.

4. Teachers should be realistic in the amount of homework they expect of students. The time required by individual students to complete assignments will influence the success of the whole homework program.

5. An increase in the amount of work required of students may not improve the quality of their education. Quality is better than quantity.

6. Young people may react negatively toward homework because of their previous experiences; therefore, the teacher may have to work extra hard to show the students how the homework will assist them in learning.

7. There should be harmony among the faculty concerning the amount and importance of homework.[8]

TYPES OF HOMEWORK

With all the different types of homework, there is no need for it to become monotonous or boring. Following are some areas that need to be explored to achieve variety.

Observing

The teacher should choose many assignments emanating from out-of-school observations. Ideas for themes, poems, stories, and other types of creative writing may be developed, as well as ideas for science projects and material for classroom discussions.

Collecting

The students may be assigned to collect samples of various types of plant or animal life, or they may save poems or readings for English class. Material gathered can include tangible objects and/or information for social studies, language arts, science, or math.[9]

Researching

In this type of homework, the students learn to use reference materials to help them find information outside of the textbooks. Research will be of great benefit to them later in life no matter what area of work they eventually pursue.

Practicing Skills

The practice of skills is probably used more than any kind of homework; therefore, it takes imaginative planning to keep it alive and challenging. Whether students are in elementary or high school, drilling in skills is essential for future success; consequently, the teacher should keep the homework from falling into "the same old stuff."[10]

Memorizing

Even though memorization is an essential part of some types of homework, an instructor should be careful that there is more than rote learning. Memory work can be given meaning if it is planned properly before being assigned. The memorization of certain facts, tables, and procedures are essential as a foundation for building a strong educational structure.

Projects

Meaningful projects can develop initiative and thought and break the ordinary stereotype homework into something original and creative. Such projects must have guidelines and must contribute to the rest of the school work, but they can be a break from the regular routine of work outside of the classroom.[11]

HOMEWORK ASSIGNMENTS

Situations may vary under which assignments are made, but there are certain essential elements that hold true for the teacher, the pupils, and the work being given.

Teacher Responsibilities Concerning the Assignment

Clarify the Assignment — Verbal instructions and explanations are not always enough for young people to understand what is expected of them. Although a teacher may think that an assignment is perfectly clear, there will always be a few who do not understand what is expected of them.

Some suggestions follow for making the assignments clear:

1. Writing such instructions for homework so that even the slow students will understand what is expected.[12]
2. Set aside a particular place on the chalkboard where assignments are always written for student reference.
3. Type out dates and assignments for the pupils.
4. Suit the style and vocabulary of the instructions for the age and experience of the group.
5. Show illustrations and even examples of the work to the young people.[13]

Anticipate Difficulties — Every new unit of learning will require the students to master new ideas. Therefore, the instructor must anticipate any possible difficulties and make suggestions to the students on how to overcome those problems.

Supervise the Beginning — After a new or difficult assignment is given, the students should be given some class time to begin work to determine if everyone is able to proceed independently.[14]

Demand that Work Be Turned in on Time — When a teacher allows students to turn in late papers, except for reasons of illness, he is encouraging young people to be lazy and irresponsible. Pupils should be penalized for late papers and still be made to do the work. After the pupils get the message that the teacher is not going to accept lateness, they will fulfill the expectations of the teacher.

Develop Good Study Habits — The teacher should use assignments for the purpose of developing good study habits, not only while the young people are doing in-class work, but also outside of class. The following are some suggestions for helping students accomplish more through their assignments: 1) read the directions before beginning, 2) concentrate on the lesson without distractions, 3) refer to previous notes taken in class, 4) follow the procedures given by the instructor, 5) do not spend too much time on any one problem, and 6) if the teacher does not object, get assistance from someone who can explain a difficulty.

Relate New Material to Past Knowledge — In order for students to acquire new knowledge, they must build on a foundation of material that is familiar to them. Young people will naturally flounder if they do not possess the tools with which they can develop new knowledge and ideas.

Suggest Availability of Needed Materials — Students may not be aware of where to find certain information; therefore, the instructor should suggest libraries, community resources, and/or individuals who can assist them in their search for the material they need. The teacher may also want to inform the students where not to waste their time in looking for other information.

Be Aware of Requirements on Students' Time — Other teachers are making assignments, too, and if each teacher requires additional homework time, the students will be overworked. Another thing to be kept in mind is that Wednesday nights should be left open so that young people may attend church services.

Arouse an Interest in the Homework — Motivation is a vital part of enabling pupils to get the most out of their assignments. Developing healthy habits and attitudes is directly related to effective motivation by the teacher.

Suggestions That Can Be Given to Students

Make Sure the Assignment Is Understood — Only the students can determine whether or not they understand the assignment. If they do not, it is their responsibility to ask questions until they know what is expected of them.

Study at Appropriate Times — "Normally," suggests Robinson, "it is better to study an assignment just after the class in which it is given, or just before the class in which it will be used if emphasis is on recitation or discussion."[15]

Assume Responsibility for Doing Own Assignment — Each student must be accountable for his own assignment. When a student copies from others, he is not gaining the knowledge he should and is culivating habits of dishonesty and deceit.

Study Every Day — It is better to study a subject every day than to wait and study for a long period of time in one day. A daily schedule will develop habits of planning, getting down to work, and concentrating.[16]

Utilize Study Helps and Available Materials — The big, black headings in a textbook are given to aid the reader in finding the important items in the chapter. Dictionaries, encyclopedias, and other reference books can enable a young person to understand certain aspects of the lesson if the materials are used at the right times.[17]

Study Efficiently — In studying over a long period of time, a young person should stop for a few minutes between chapters or between subjects. He will receive renewed energy if he gets up, stretches, and relaxes for a bit. The body becomes tired and dull by continuously sitting in the same place for over an hour.

CAUTIONS CONCERNING HOMEWORK

Check Homework

When the students take the time to do the assignment that the teacher has made, the least the teacher can do is to check it. Everyone loses when the teacher does not check the homework: 1) the students realize the teacher is inconsistent; 2) the next time an assignment is given, the young people are less likely to do it; and 3) parents who know the teacher did not bother to check the work lose confidence in the teacher and the school.

Learning and Homework

"Don't expect homework to teach a student who is not learning properly in the classroom."[18] If the pupil is not able to comprehend the work in class, chances are he will not get the material when he attempts the task at home.

Punishment

Homework should never be given for punishment. Certainly pupils will not always have a positive attitude toward having to do homework, but they will sour on outside work if a teacher disciplines a class by giving additional work.

Busywork

Homework should not be given if there is no justifiable reason for giving it. To dole out busywork just for the sake of having the pupils doing something will create a negative response on the part of the students.[19]

Help from Others

Hoover says that if a teacher is not careful, he will be grading and giving credit for work that has been done by "parents, neighbors, older siblings, or anyone who happened to be available."[20] Therefore, it might be advisable for a teacher merely to check to see if the pupils have their work completed and then go over the material with the students in class, having them check their own work to see if it is right or wrong. At that time the pupils should be allowed to ask questions as to why their answers differed from the correct ones.

PARENTS AND HOMEWORK

The parents of children who attend private schools show a higher level of expectation along scholastic lines. These parents usually provide more than a pleasant environment for doing homework; "they become partners in the work to be done."[21] Because homework is required in most Christian schools, parents get involved in one way or another. Dr. Benjamin Fine gives these suggestions for parents desiring to help with their children's homework:

Remember that children should enjoy a quiet, happy atmosphere in the evening.

Don't get so emotionally involved in your children's success or failure that you make them nervous and tense.

Don't do the lion's share of their homework. It is their work, not yours, that the teacher wants to evaluate.

Don't confuse them by teaching them your methods of solving long division or other arithmetic problems. Many schools use a new approach today.

Check their homework after it is finished to see whether there are any careless mistakes. Significant errors will need the teacher's attention.

Help them select topics for themes; help find books, pamphlets, and magazine articles that they need for their research. You may even help collect material for projects, although children should assume the major responsibility for getting the items.

It is valuable for you . . . to meet with your children's teachers and to take an active interest in all their school problems. Homework is only one part of their school life.[22]

PROJECTS

Whatever subject a person teaches, he will find that assigning projects is beneficial. Projects fall into the following categories: 1) long-term
projects, which may last for a semester; 2) short-term projects, which may
be for six weeks; 3) group projects, and 4) individual projects. Some projects may culminate with an oral presentation, but not all projects need to
have the students explain their material verbally in front of the class.

Many teachers take advantage of the creative ability of students
who do not perform well on tests, but find working with their hands more
enjoyable. Teachers may choose to grade these activities in such a way as
to reward students for the efforts as well as their finished products, but
whatever the completed work may be, the students should be allowed to
show and explain to the class what they have done.[23]

Regardless of the project, the teacher should have check points
along the way to determine if the pupils are keeping up with their projects.
For instance, with a research paper the instructor should have deadlines
for the thesis statement, bibliography cards, note cards, outline, rough
draft, and finally the finished product. If there is no checking up along the
way, most young people will wait until the last week to accomplish what
takes weeks to do.

WAYS OF CHECKING HOMEWORK

As has been mentioned previously, there is nothing more discourag-
ing to students than to find that after they have spent time working on
their homework, the teacher does not bother to check it. Checking homework is vital for effective teaching, and the following are suggested ways
that it might be done.

1. The teacher may simply walk around the room with his gradebook and look to see that the work is finished. He is not determining if it is right or wrong; that will be decided when the material is gone over in class.
2. He may have the pupils, a few at a time, bring their work up to
   his desk. After the students know what order they appear on the
   class roll, they can follow in order without any lapse of time.
3. Students may hold up their work when their names are called,
   but the teacher should warn them to hold up the right papers.
4. The teacher may have the pupils simply answer, "yes" or "no" as
   to whether or not the assignment is completed and on their
   desks.
5. Still another way is to require the young people to exchange
   papers and check the work as the teacher goes over it.
6. The least favorable way is for the teacher to collect the home-

work to check it himself. Not only can this be very time-consuming, but the young people will not be aware of what they are missing in the assignment.

Whatever means the teacher uses to make sure the assignment is complete, he should check in class to see that the homework is done correctly so that the pupils may know what they are missing.

CONCLUSION

It is difficult to prescribe an exact amount of time that pupils should spend on their homework for a specific subject. The amount of time will certainly vary with each student, but on the average, a young person should not spend over two and one half hours on his homework for all classes combined. After all, every teacher should be striving for the qualitative rather than the quantitative elements of homework.[24]

FOOTNOTES

[1]Benjamine Fine and Lillian Fine, *How to Get the Best Education for Your Child* (New York: G.P. Putman's Sons, 1959), p. 136.

[2]William T. Gruh and Harl R. Douglas, *The Modern Junior High School* (New York: The Ronald Press Company, 1947), p. 215.

[3]H.G. Rickover, *Education and Freedom* (New York: E.P. Dutton and Co., Inc., 1959), p. 119.

[4]Thomas J. Whalen, "Homework," compiled by James A. Johnson and Roger C. Anderson in *Secondary Student Teaching Readings* (Glenview, Illinois: Scott, Foresman and Company, 1971), p. 136.

[5]Ralph W. Tyler, "The Problems and Possibilities of Educational Evolution," *The Schools and the Challenge of Innovation* (New York: McGraw-Hill Book Company, 1969), p. 83.

[6]Max Rafferty, *Max Rafferty on Education* (New York: The Devin-Adair Company, 1968), p. 84.

[7]Kenneth H. Hoover, *Learning and Teaching in the Secondary School* (Boston: Allyn and Bacon, Inc., 1965), pp. 504-505.

[8]Sterling G. Callahan, *Successful Teaching in Secondary Schools* (Glenview, Illinois: Scott, Foresman and Company 1971), p. 200.

[9]Grace Langdon and Irving W. Stout, *Homework* (New York: The John Day Company, 1969), pp. 52-53.

[10]Ibid., p. 54.

[11]Ibid., pp. 55-56.

[12]Jenny Gray, *The Teacher's Survival Guide* (Palo Alto, California: Fearon Publishers, 1967), p. 18.

[13]Nelson L. Bossing, *Teaching in Secondary Schools*, 3rd. ed., (Boston: Houghton Mifflin Company, 1952), p. 302.

[14]Gail M. Inlow, *Maturity in High School* (Englewood Cliffs, New Jersey: Prentice-Hall, Inc., 1963), p. 166.

[15]Francis P. Robinson, *Effective Study* (New York: Harper and Row, Publishers, 1961), p. 76.

[16]Ibid.

[17]Inlow, p. 166.

[18]Kenneth T. Henson, *Secondary Teaching Methods* (Lexington, Massachusetts: D.C. Heath and Company, 1981), p. 167.

[19]Callahan, p. 203.

[20]Hoover, p. 510.

[21]George D. Stoddard, *The Out-Look for American Education* (Carbondale, Ill.: Southern Illinois University Press, 1974), p. 91.

[22]Benjamine Fine, *Your Child and School* (New York: The Macmillan Company, 1965), p. 103.

[23]Henson, p. 166.

[24]Whalen, p. 137.

QUESTIONS AND PROBLEMS

1. What is your philosophy concerning the use of homework?

2. Why is it that first year teachers usually have difficulty with the amount of homework that should be given?

3. Do you think that some subjects are more important than others, and therefore, those teachers who teach those subjects should be allowed to give more homework? Explain.

4. In this chapter, which of the types of homework is probably used more than the others? Which is used the least? Can you give reasons for these answers?

5. What do you think about pupils receiving help with their homework from relatives or other students? If your answer is in the affirmative, what precautions should be given?

6. How much should homework count as far as a final grade is concerned?

7. Why should teachers never throw homework papers in the waste paper basket while the students are in the room?

8. In thinking back over your school experiences, are there any assignments that you remember as being helpful and enjoyable? Were there some you considered needless and meaningless?

Evaluation
And
Testing

Chapter 8

VIII
EVALUATION AND TESTING

Man is an evaluative being. He evaluates his possessions and those of his neighbors, the various elements of his environment, his fellow man, and even himself. The practice of evaluation is as old as recorded history. The adult individual in our society is evaluated in his various roles on the job, in the community, and at home. Likewise, the young of the species are evaluated in their various roles within the school, the community, and the home.[1]

The word "evaluation" comes from the root word "value." To evaluate means to judge the worth of a performance or product.[2] Therefore, evaluation is the process by which a human being passes judgment on the value of anything. The individual's judgment depends upon the values that he possesses, and those values will come from all of his past experiences and relationships.[3] The Christian teacher must make sure that his values are derived from the Word of God and directed by the Holy Spirit in order for his judgments to be fair and effective.

Evaluation includes measurement (testing). When a teacher measures what the students know, he has only evaluated a small portion of what has been taught in the classroom. Testing is usually based upon the cognitive, whereas evaluation involves a qualitative judgment founded upon a set of values. Evaluation is much broader than measurement, for it includes many things, while testing encompasses only such matters as constructing examinations, administering them, and grading. For example, using the results of test scores to assist students and help them to improve would fall into the area of evaluation.[4]

THE PURPOSE OF EVALUATION

When a teacher tests or evaluates, he should have certain purposes in mind. Evaluation will assist the teacher in relationships with students, parents, administration, guidance and counseling, and himself.

The Pupils

Evaluation and testing are important to pupils for various reasons. When the teacher provides information regarding classroom measurements, the students are able to assess themselves in relation to one another. However, the teacher must guide the students in developing proper assessments in order to acquire proper self-concepts and realistic goals.[5] In order to provide guidance toward healthy attitudes and habits, the Christian teacher must be constantly directed by the Holy Spirit.

The Parents

The teacher must be in touch with parents in order for them to be aware of their child's progress not only in academics, but also in such matters as values, attitudes, appreciations, and other such affective traits. Parents want to know how their child is measuring up in these areas, and a systematic use of evaluation in the classroom will present the teacher with an objective picture to relate to the parents.[6] After receiving such information, parents are in a better position to assist their youngsters to attain the goals they believe God wants their children to attain.

The Administration

Effective evaluation on the part of the teacher provides the school with the necessary information on which to make decisions concerning placements, groupings, and promotion of pupils. From the material turned in by the teachers, the administration is able to identify strengths and weaknesses in the curriculum, to appraise special programs in the institution, and to determine if the goals of the school have been met.[7]

The Counselor

The results of proper evaluation will help counselors assist pupils with educational and vocational decisions, direct them to appropriate curriculum choices, and guide them in solving personal and social problems. "The more comprehensive the picture of the pupil's strengths and limitations in various areas, the greater the likelihood of effective guidance and counseling,"[8] remarks Gronlund.

The Teacher

Thorough evaluation is important as far as the teacher is concerned because it permits him to analyze whether or not he has accomplished what he endeavored to achieve. If learning is to progress at the maximum, the teacher must be aware of the students' progress toward the learning goals. When difficulties arise from the students' lack of understanding, reteaching may be necessary. Conversely, when the students master the concepts, the teacher should introduce enrichment experiences for them. The Christian worker must continually assess the students' achievements in order to determine what adjustments need to be made in the program.[9]

TYPES OF EVALUATION

The main source of evaluation in the classroom is the teacher. Silberman says, "He is called upon continuously to make judgments of students' work and behavior and to communicate that judgment to students and to others."[10] But whatever techniques of appraisal are taken, the more the teacher uses, the better will be the outcome. Major tests and occasional quizzes are obvious methods of evaluating young people's accomplishments; however, there are other means at the teacher's disposal.

Informal Observation

Inlow believes that informal observation is the primary type of evaluation.[11] This type of observation is very demanding and includes such matters as noticing signs of restlessness, insisting on eye contact, noting social behavior, responding to inattention, reacting to academic responses, and determining emotional pressures. These things and more come under the appraisal of the teacher who desires to evaluate his students through means other than written tests.[12]

Formal Observation

Unlike the informal observation, the formal is a planned implementation of the observational technique, using the anecdotal recording of actions for further study of a particular pupil.[13]

Written Projects

Written work takes on many forms in the classroom. A teacher uses a completely different avenue of appraisal to evaluate homework, term papers, essays, short compositions, or any other written materials.

Oral Methods

Performance and personality are often manifested in the oral responses of pupils. The informal question, the more voluntary recitation, the spontaneous interaction within a class discussion, and the formal report are all examples of things students say that can be evaluated.

Other Means of Observation

Still other means of observation open to the teacher include board work, academic records, interviews, health records, home visits, autobiographies, projects, standardized tests, and cumulative records. Thus, tests are not the only means of evaluation. Indeed the use of tests is insufficient to arrive at a complete profile of the whole child, for almost everything the youngster does is able to be evaluated.

TESTING AS A PART OF EVALUATION

Buffington says concerning tests:

> Tests are necessary to describe levels of knowledge and to assist in making placement decisions. They are capable of motivating via feedback. So it is important to develop a healthy, positive attitude toward examinations. As classroom tests are mastered, they serve as "trial runs" for other, more difficult life tests.[14]

Certainly many tests, trials, and crises occur during the lifetime of any person; therefore, a youngster in school should be taught to face his responsibilities in preparing for examinations, reports, and other obligations.

It has been conservatively estimated that in twelve years of elementary and secondary education alone, a student will take approximately 2,600 tests and quizzes; college midterms and final examinations over a four-year period will add another one hundred exams to the total.[15] Therefore, tests are an important aspect of the student's life and should not be treated lightly by the pupil or the teacher.

Purposes of Teacher-Made Tests

Schwartz and Tiedeman give the purposes of the teacher-made tests. Those tests permit the teacher to:
1. Measure and evaluate student progress in the light of classroom goals.
2. Motivate students to learn specific information as well as general knowledge.
3. Determine the strengths and weaknesses of the individual and the group.
4. Check more frequently on the pupil's progress.
5. Gather specific information for purposes of reporting.
6. Modify curriculum and instructional procedures if tests indicate a need.[16]

General Suggestions for Classroom Tests

In constructing tests, the teacher should keep the following guidelines in mind:

1. Avoid vague and ambiguous questions.
2. Test only material that the class is expected to know.
3. Make a key for every test.
4. Do not lift questions directly from the textbook.
5. Avoid tricky questions.
6. Make the questions as brief and concise as possible.
7. Determine length of test by the age of the pupils.
8. Group similar types of questions together.
9. Teach students how to take various types of tests.
10. Limit test to available time.
11. Make scoring of the test as easy as possible.
12. Keep a copy of every test.[17]

Characteristics of Objective Type Questions

Objective questions fall into two basic categories: 1) those questions that require the student to supply the answer, and 2) those that require him to choose an answer from a number of alternatives. These two groups fall basically into four types of objective test items: 1) short-answer, 2) true-false, 3) matching, and 4) multiple-choice. The following are suggestions in construction of each.

Short-Answer

1. The teacher should only require brief and definite answers.
2. Statements should not be taken directly from the text.
3. A direct question is better than an incomplete statement.
4. Too many blanks should not be used in one item.[18]
5. The length of the blank should not indicate the answer.[19]

True-False

1. Broad, general statements should be avoided.
2. Trivial statements should not be used.
3. Negative statements are too difficult to figure out.[20]
4. The number of true statements and false statements should be approximately equal in number.[21]
5. If opinion is called for, the teacher should state in the question whose opinion he wants.[22]

Matching

1. Only homogeneous material should be used in a set.[23]
2. The list of responses should be arranged in logical order.
3. The directions for matching should be indicated.
4. All items for one matching exercise should be on one page.

5. The shorter responses should be brief and placed on the right.
6. There should be more responses on the right than on the left.[24]

Multiple-Choice

1. The stem should be meaningful and should present a problem.
2. All of the alternatives should be grammatically consistent with the stem of the item.
3. All distracters should be plausible.
4. The length of the alternatives should not provide a clue to the answer.[25]
5. The correct answer should appear in each of the alternatives approximately an equal number of times but in random order.[26]

Suggestions for Constructing and Scoring Essay Questions

Constructing Essay Questions

1. The teacher should use essay questions to measure thinking skills, organization of ideas, and expression of thoughts.
2. Each question should be worded so that the students know exactly what is expected of them.
3. The approximate time limit for each question should be indicated.
4. Pupils should not be allowed to choose the essay questions they wish to answer.[27]

Scoring Essay Questions

1. The teacher should grade all answers to one question before going on to the next question.
2. By trying not to look at the student's name while grading, the grader will remain unprejudiced.
3. Irrelevant items inserted by the pupil should not influence the teacher in his evaluation.
4. The teacher should prepare an outline of the correct answers before the test for the purpose of grading.[28]

Preparation for the Test

Eble believes that because most young people desire to make good grades, tests may be used for learning, motivating, and measuring. All three of these purposes are useful for the teacher.[29] When students are aware of their strengths and weaknesses, Sorenson says, they will "work harder and more intelligently."[30]

The test should include the major topics that have been emphasized in class. The teacher needs to be careful, balanced, and precise in designing the examination.[31] He should announce tests several days in advance and remind the students of the test each succeeding day, so that the pupils will have enough time to prepare. The teacher should also give specific instructions beforehand concerning any materials that students will need to bring to class with them.[32]

Before Handing Out Tests

The instructor should give attention to certain matters before administering the tests. For instance, if the students are to use any equipment such as a ruler, compass, or cover-sheet, those items should be on their desks before the tests are passed out. Wall maps, charts, or other items that might give clues to answers should be removed from sight. Perhaps a change of seating might be arranged to enable the young people to sit in every other row.

Still another thing the teacher needs to do before distributing tests is to warn the pupils concerning cheating. The students should be told that all study aids — whether on notebook paper, cards, or anything else — must be put out of sight. Without special permission, young ladies should not open their purses during the test, nor should the young men pull items from their pockets. The teacher must be careful not to say that an individual caught cheating will be expelled, since a teacher does not have the authority to expel students.

He should tell the students that if they have a question, they should raise their hands and wait for the teacher to come to them. A young person should never get out of his seat nor should he talk out during the examination.

After all of these preliminaries have been taken care of, the teacher should lead in prayer asking the Lord to enable everyone to do his best and not to yield to any temptation to cheat.

Passing Out the Tests

When passing out the tests, the teacher should make sure that every pupil receives a clear, readable paper. Walton writes, legible test papers will "reduce the excuses for asking questions during the examination and for misunderstandings."[33] The instructor should also take care not to pass out more tests than the number of students in the class, and if there is a second sheet, that everyone receives one. In addition to these matters, he should go over the directions for the test unless understanding the directions is part of the test.[34]

Administering the Test

During the test it is advisable that the instructor walk around the room. Such vigilance will do two things: first, anyone who might be tempted to cheat will have less opportunity; and, secondly, the teacher will be more accessible for any questions. When the student calls attention to an error on the test, the teacher must give the correction to the whole class.

Sometimes a pupil will ask a question that will give a clue to the answer when the question is asked aloud; therefore, the pupils must be cautioned as to what they ask. Another problem to be avoided is that of allowing students to get out of their seats during the test. By not allowing young people to leave their desks during the test, the teacher will eliminate a great deal of distractions and the possibility of their looking at answers. Needless to say, the teacher should never leave the room while administering a test.

Collecting Test Papers

"To increase smoothness of operation and to save time, establish a testing routine which students can learn to follow automatically,"[35] advises Samalonis. When pupils have finished their tests, they need to know what is expected of them. The teacher may require them to bring their tests to him or to place their tests face down on their desks until he picks them up. After completing a test, a young person should not open his textbook or look at his notes for fear that someone around him might see answers to the test. The students may also give their tests to the teacher as they leave the room but the teacher should make sure that he has received a test from everyone.

Grading Test Papers

The teacher should correct and return the test papers as soon as possible. When he does return them to the class, he should explain the correct answer to each question. Such a procedure shows the pupils their errors, and contributes to their understanding of the material. It also reduces the number of questions from individual students who would seek explanations as to why their answers were incorrect. An effective technique that the teacher may use in going over a test, is to call on students who gave good answers, asking them to read their answer to the rest of the class. This not only shows the rest of the pupils that a complete, correct answer was possible to a question, but also may serve as an incentive to other members of the class to strive for such answers on future tests.[36]

Never should a teacher's personal feelings toward a student influence the way he grades that young person's paper. It would be inexcusable for a Christian teacher to be influenced for or against a pupil, for he must always be "honest, open, and fair."[37] Young people respond to teachers who are fair and interested in them. Not only do the students respond to the fair teacher, but Page discovered that when a teacher not only marked tests with a letter or numerical grade but also made some comment of praise on their papers, the students improved on their tests that followed.[38]

The Problem of Cheating

Whether in a Christian school or non-Christian school, the problem of cheating will occur sooner or later. Walton believes that a teacher should take every precaution to make sure that it does not happen:

> . . . by walking up and down the aisles, and standing in the back of the room, seating the students so that one seat separates any two of them taking the test; and keeping test questions securely out of the reach of students before the examination.[39]

When the teacher has the students grade one another's papers, he should institute certain safeguards.

1. The way the students exchange papers should be different every time; otherwise, best friends will keep grading each other's papers and may help one another out.
2. The grader should write his name at the bottom of the paper.
3. A wiggly line should be drawn in any space where there is no written answer.
4. The grader could be required to bring a red pen or pencil to class for the purpose of grading.
5. Students might be penalized for the improper grading of other students' papers.
6. After the papers are graded by the students, the papers should be returned to the owners.[40]

Every teacher must be very cautious about making accusations concerning cheating unless he has solid proof. However, says Walton, "if students are caught cheating on examinations, and if the evidence is clear and incontrovertible, usually, no less a penalty than failure on that examination should be exacted."[41]

GRADING AND REPORT CARDS

The administration usually permits the teacher to decide his own formula for averaging the students' grades. How much value tests are going to count and what percentage of the final grade will be allotted to homework, reports, quizzes, themes, projects, and class discussions must be determined by the teacher.

Determining a Grade

The percentage assigned to various elements of school work will vary from subject to subject. For instance, more oral exercises will take place in language class than in chemistry class. Drayer says, "Similarly, some teachers assign major projects, while others do not; in some cases, more homework is given than in others; some courses include laboratory work, but many do not."[42] In the final analysis, then, the grade must be determined by the teacher himself.

A possible guide for averaging grades might be the following: approximately 20% for the final examination, 40% given to major tests, 10% assigned to homework, 10% for oral reports, 10% for special projects, and 10% for class discussions.[43]

> A system of grading such as the above has several advantages. Since it embraces several elements, the student must do well in all phases in order to merit an evaluation of "superior." This fact encourages the student to be active continuously, rather than to coast along until time for an infrequent test.[44]

When a teacher has arrived at a grade in a conscientious and careful manner, he should not allow a student to influence him to change it. If, however, he has made an error in his calculations, he should by all means alter the grade that was previously recorded.

Inlow writes, "A grade should never be used punitively or regarded as a token either of respectability or unrespectability."[45] Indeed when a conduct grade is given, it should be separate from the academic grade, and the two should not be mixed. In addition to this safeguard, the teacher must not disclose a student's grade to any other pupil or to any parent other than the student's own parent.

Reporting to Parents

Finally, report cards should not be the only means of contact between the teacher and the parents. The more contacts between the school and the home, the healthier will be the relationship of all concerned. Notes, open house, telephone calls, parent-teacher conferences, and three-week reports are some of the ways that teachers can keep in touch with parents. Maintaining a friendly and professional open door policy with parents will provide an important means of selling the school's program and will also be the means of enlisting parental help for their child.

CONCLUSION

Teachers, students, parents, and the school are helped when the teacher implements a well balanced process of evaluation in the classroom. Obviously, Christian experiences and Christian living cannot always be measured by a mere human being, but with the help of the Holy Spirit, the Christian teacher can endeavor to be fair and just in his evaluations for the purpose of developing character in the lives of the students. Eavey says,

> Christian teaching has been defined as the guiding of "activity by which persons live and grow in the Christian faith-life." All the knowledge we can get is bound together by faith. Christ is central in all of life and everything, for the Christian teacher is bound together in Him. The genius of Christian teaching is that knowledge ends in Christ.

The teacher's purpose is not merely to present the Bible. That is important. But what is more important is that the teacher impart Christ. For
doing this, the Christian character of the teacher is paramount.[46]

FOOTNOTES

[1]John Clark Marshall and Loyde Wessley Hales, *Essentials of Testing* (Reading, Massachusetts: Addison-Wesley Publishing Company, 1972), p. 132.

[2]William L. Carter, Carl W. Hansen, and Margaret S. McKim, *Learning to Teach in the Secondary School* (New York: The MacMillan Company, 1962), p. 311.

[3]William M. Alexander and Paul M. Halverson, *Effective Teaching in Secondary Schools* (New York: Rinehart and Company, 1956), p. 393.

[4]Kenneth T. Henson, *Secondary Teaching Methods* (Lexington, Massachusetts: D.C. Heath and Company, 1981), p. 337.

[5]Marshall, p. 133.

[6]Norman E. Gronlund, *Measurement and Evaluation in Teaching,* 4th ed., (New York: MacMillan Publishing Co., Inc. 1981), p. 12.

[7]Ibid.

[8]Ibid.

[9]Marshall, p. 133.

[10]Charles E. Silberman, *Crisis in the Classroom* (New York: Random House, 1970), p. 138.

[11]Gail M. Inlow, *Maturity in the High School Teaching* (Englewood Cliffs, New Jersey: Prentice-Hall, Inc., 1963), p. 261.

[12]Ibid.

[13]Gronlund, p. 435.

[14]Perry W. Buffington, "Of Tests and Techniques," *Sky,* May 1981, p. 32.

[15]Ibid., p. 30

[16]Alfred Schwartz and S.C. Tiedeman, *Evaluating Student Progress in the Secondary School* (New York: Longman, Green and Co., David McKay Co., 1957), p. 110.

[17]Kenneth H. Hoover, *Learning and Teaching in the Secondary School* (Boston: Allyn and Bacon, Inc., 1964), p. 454.

[18]Gronlund, pp. 159-162.

[19]Hoover, p. 454.

[20]Ibid., pp. 167-168.

[21]Arnold J. Lien, *Measurement and Evaluation of Learning,* 3rd ed. (Dubuque, Iowa: Wm. C. Brown Company Pub., 1976), p. 218.

[22]Gronlund, p. 169.

[23]Lien, p. 224.

[24]Gronlund, pp. 173-175.

[25]Ibid., pp. 189-196.

[26]Lien, p. 222.

[27]Gronlund, pp. 229-232.

[28]Ibid., pp. 234-235.

[29]Kenneth E. Eble, *The Craft of Teaching* (Washington: Jossey-Bass Publishers, 1976), p. 109.

[30]Herbert Sorenson, *Psychology in Education* (New York: McGraw-Hill Book Co., 1964), p. 413.

[31]Eble, p. 109.

[32]John Walton, *Toward Better Teaching in the Secondary Schools* (Boston: Allyn and Bacon, 1966), p. 247.

[33]Ibid., p. 247.

[34]Ibid.

[35]Bernice L. Samalonis, *Methods and Materials for Today's High School* (New York: Van Nostrand Reinhold Co., 1970), p. 139.

[36]Adam M. Drayer, *Problems and Methods in High School Teaching* (Boston: D.C. Heath and Company, 1963), p. 152.

[37]Eble, p. 109.

[38]Ellis B. Page, "Teacher Comments and Student Performance: A Seventy-four Classroom Experiment in School Motivation," *Journal of Educational Psychology,* 48 (August 1958), pp. 173-181.

[39]Walton, p. 298.

[40]Ibid., p. 247.

[41]Ibid., p. 299.

[42]Drayer, p. 145.

[43]Ibid., p. 146.

[44]Ibid.

[45]Inlow, p. 335.

[46]C.B. Eavey, *The Art of Effective Teaching* (Grand Rapids, Michigan: Zondervan Publishing House, 1956), p. 266.

QUESTIONS AND PROBLEMS

1. Has your course in Tests and Measurements in college helped you in your teaching? Explain.

2. Have you ever had a teacher in high school or college who never returned your tests or other papers? What is your opinion of such a teacher? Why do you think a teacher would do things like that?

3. Would you agree with the statement, "If cheating occurs in the classroom, it is the teacher's fault?" Give reasons to support your answer.

4. Discuss ways that you have seen or heard of young people cheating in class.

5. Name various ways a teacher evaluates young people in his/her classroom other than tests and quizzes.

6. Give reasons why parents need to be forewarned of their child's poor grades and/or improper conduct.

7. What do you think about appointing monitors and having them report misconduct of pupils their own age? Explain.

8. Do you think the school should have students evaluate their teachers? Explain.

9. Do you use a grading system that is different than the one described under "Determining a Grade?" What do you use?

Enthusiastic Teaching

Chapter 9

IX
ENTHUSIASTIC TEACHING

God does not believe in halfheartedness, for He commands His children ". . . whatsoever ye do, do all to the glory of God."[1] He says again in Colossians 3:17, "And whatsoever ye do in word or deed, do all in the name of the Lord Jesus Christ." The Christian who obeys the Lord in these verses will not only be controlled by the Holy Spirit, but he will be an excited servant of the Lord. His life will be controlled by the Spirit, be led by the Spirit, and have the fervor and energy of the Spirit. In other words, a person will show enthusiasm in the work of God.

And why would the Lord not desire that man be enthusiastic? Did He not promise to be with Israel ". . . with My whole heart and with My whole soul"?[2] As Young says, "Here we are brought face to face with the kindling fact that God is a God of enthusiasm. He is thrilled through and through with splendid passion. He is every way and forever 'a consuming fire.' "[3] Moses assured the children of Israel, "Fear ye not, stand still, and see the salvation of the Lord" (Exodus 14:13). Later, Isaiah also declared concerning the impossible deliverance of God's people from their iron oppressor, ". . . the zeal of the Lord of Hosts shall do this."[4]

God in Christ is always a God of enthusiasm. How intense He is! How He prays! The fervor of His prayers is never chilled. How He meditates! His inexplorable thoughts breathe themselves through eternity. How He commends the good, the brave, the true, the beautiful! How He denounces the wrong, the base, the insincere! The Christ of the New Testament is the Jehovah of the Old Testament, in white-hot enthusiasm, as in everything, august, and gentle, and lovely.

Enthusiasm must surely be an essential of a true theology. One cannot conceive of an impassionate God. An apathetic God would depress the universe. The very idea and etymology of the word "enthusiasm" involves God. All noble fervor is Divine in its origination. An ancient Greek finely described enthusiasm as "a god within." And such all grand enthusiasm is, and must be evermore.[5]

The true ideal for man is to imitate God's enthusiasm for the lost to be saved, for His love to be shown, and for His children to grow in grace and truth. Christian teachers need to win their students to the Lord; they must demonstrate Christ's love by the way they act; and they should be enthusiastic in their teaching, in order for young people to learn the myriad knowledge of His universe.

Webster defines "enthusiasm" as "inspiration by a god or other superhuman power; divine possession."[6] The word is derived from the Greek "enthousiasmos" which means "to be inspired." Certainly the Christian teacher is possessed by the Divine, and because the Holy Spirit of God dwells within him, he should be inspired by a "superhuman power." The dictionary continues its definition of enthusiasm as "a strong excitement of feeling on behalf of a cause or a subject: ardent zeal or interest."[7] How descriptive of the enthusiastic teacher. Every Christian should strive to be an enthusiastic teacher.

General MacArthur wrote:

> You are as young as your faith, as old as your doubt; as young as your self-confidence, as old as your fear; as young as your hope, as old as your despair. Years may wrinkle your skin, but to give up enthusiasm wrinkles up your soul.[8]

Rosenshine gives an example of an experimental study in which twenty teachers of sixth and seventh grade pupils were asked to manipulate teacher enthusiasm as the independent variable. Each teacher taught lessons on ancient Egypt and Rome. Instructions were given to each teacher to teach one lesson with enthusiasm, that is, "in such a manner as to convey to his pupils the impression that he was enthusiastic about the ideas and illustrative materials of the lesson and subject covered by the lesson."[9] Each teacher was also instructed to teach some lessons with indifference, that is, "in such a manner as to convey to the group a feeling that he had an indifferent attitude about the ideas, etc."[10] After the teachers taught each lesson, Rosenshine explains that the students took a 102-item, multiple-choice test. "The class mean for the lesson which was taught with enthusiasm, whether that lesson was the lecture on Rome or on Egypt, was higher for nineteen of the twenty classes than the mean of the lesson presented with indifference."[11] These results suggest that there are significant pupil achievements as a result of lessons taught in an enthusiastic manner as opposed to lessons presented in a dull, routine style.

Since teacher enthusiasm has a significant influence on the students' learning and attitudes, it is important that every Christian teacher do his utmost to develop in this area. Mastin believes, "The attitudes which teachers have toward the topic, materials, and ideas which they present to their classes do influence the factual learning of the pupils in their classes, and the attitudes of those pupils."[12] Therefore, teachers must get excited about the subjects they present to the students.

Preparing lessons and being knowledgeable about the material are not enough; teachers must cultivate enthusiasm. Yes, instructors should be enthusiastic even in those subjects that are not their favorites. "Tremendous" Jones believes, "If I don't get excited about what I don't like to do, I don't get much that I do like to be excited about."[13]

An enthusiasm based on knowledge of the material will break down a negative resistance on the part of students; however, the teacher's lack of excitement will prevent him from realizing his full potential. Sanford and Yeager write, "Indifference, sluggishness, lifelessness, and plain laziness must be avoided by speakers who aim at success. A vital part of their mental equipment must be enthusiasm."[14] If an individual's feeling comes from within as a result of a thorough knowledge of the material and a genuine desire for the pupils to learn, then his animation will be sincere. If on the other hand, he must force his enthusiasm, it will probably appear artificial.[15]

Hegarty says that genuine enthusiasm in teaching will bring results for the following reasons:

1. The teacher's ideas will seem better because there is excitement in what he is saying.
2. Enthusiasm gives assurance to the students in that they feel they are doing the right thing because the teacher is so excited about what he is saying.
3. The teacher comes across as an interesting person to follow. Most everyone wants to associate with an individual who appears to know where he is going.
4. Enthusiasm is contagious; it is unknowingly transferred to the young people in the classroom. Students will get excited about the material because the teacher is excited.
5. An individual's enthusiasm will set him apart from the crowd. Very few teachers are excited about their work, but those who are stand out among their colleagues.[16]

EIGHT CHARACTERISTICS OF AN ENTHUSIASTIC TEACHER

Collins lists eight characteristics of enthusiasm demonstrated in the classroom from a study she conducted:

1. The teacher's voice had variations from rapid, excited speech to a sudden whisper, and the teacher's pitch fluctuated in pleasing tones.
2. The eyes of the enthusiastic teacher were shining and dancing. Frequently they were opened wide with eyebrows raised. At all times there was eye contact with the class so that everyone felt that he was important.
3. Gestures were frequently demonstrated with movements of the body, head, arms, hands, and face. Some of the gestures were sweeping motions, but all were genuine and real.
4. Movements of the body were large with exaggerations and changes of pace. Never was there moving about just for the sake of moving.
5. The facial expressions of the instructor were vibrant and demonstrative denoting a variety of moods such as surprise, sadness, joy, thoughtfulness, awe, or excitement. Facial expressions that are truly felt by the teacher will hold the attention of the pupils and will create interest in the subject matter.
6. Proper word selections that were very descriptive and greatly varied gave color and action to what was said.
7. The teacher's acceptance of the students' ideas and feelings enabled them to want to participate and contribute to the class. The teacher demonstrated his acceptance with vigor and animation through praise, encouragement, or clarifying in a nonthreatening manner and at all times responded to the young people.
8. The overall energy of the teacher was exuberant with a high degree of vitality and spirit throughout the lesson.[17]

FOUR BASIC FUNDAMENTALS FOR ENTHUSIASM

Four fundamentals are involved in the development of an enthusiastic educational personality:

1. Knowledge of the subject gives self-assurance, which in turn develops security in an honest presentation of the material. "Enthusiasm," says Mr. B., "is knowledge on fire."[18] No one is a born teacher; he must work at becoming a better one. However, no teacher can be an enthusiastic teacher without knowledge, for knowledge enables the instructor to unlock the doors of the mind.

2. Good parent-teacher relationships will enable the teacher to have the proper outlook on life because he has learned submission to authority and will be able to guide young people to have the same attitude.

3. The teacher who has good health is fortunate. Good health results in energy, which sparks enthusiasm.

4. Happy home relationships produce a pleasing personality which begets confidence and inspires other people to do what is expected of them. Others usually react to an individual as he reacts to them. If a person acts small, he can expect to have small influence with others. If, on the other hand, a teacher has respect for those with whom he lives and if he takes an unselfish interest in other people, he will develop characteristics which will produce a genuine and sincere enthusiasm.[19]

HOW TO BECOME AN ENTHUSIASTIC TEACHER

"To become enthusiastic does not mean becoming hysterical or overly emotional," explains Henson, "yet you cannot afford to be nonchalant or just mildly interested in the lesson."[20] Some teachers who are considered successful were not originally endowed with natural enthusiasm, but by working at it, they have developed into effective, excited instructors. Certainly, these all believed that enthusiasm was important.

Believe the Subject Is Important

Drayer says,

A teacher cannot hope to generate interest in his subject unless he is convinced that it is very important and very interesting. Even though enthusiasm is catching, it is evident that something must be transmitted before it can be received. A teacher must regard his subject as alive, and indispensable for the proper development of the individual. If he feels that way about it, the probability is high that he will transmit some of that feeling to his students.[21]

An ordinary lesson presented enthusiastically is often more successful than an intelligent lesson delivered in a tired, dull manner. Knowledge is not enough. A teacher must display a positive attitude toward himself, his subject, and his students. By having self-confidence, an individual will exude positiveness and will convince the young people in his class that the lesson is important.

When a teacher lectures on a topic which he finds uninteresting, he will reflect that lack of interest in his presentation; therefore, he must exhibit a confidence toward the material whether he is interested in it or not in order to convince the pupils of its importance.[22]

Act Enthusiastic

Authors Hill and Stone write: "To be enthusiastic ACT enthusiastic. The emotions are not immediately subject to reason, but they are immediately subject to action. And the action can be physical or it can be mental."[23] It is true that by merely walking in a brisk manner and carrying himself with confidence, the teacher will give an impression of enthusiasm. Young people will respond academically to the instructor who is animated and who gestures and moves about the class with purpose.[24]

Carnegie puts it this way: "This is the day of dramatization. Merely stating a truth isn't enough. The truth has to be made vivid, interesting, dramatic."[25] Students will remember the teacher's statements much longer if the teacher acts enthusiastic about the material.

Put Enthusiasm in Your Voice

A person's voice is one of the strongest aids in showing enthusiasm to others, as long as it reflects sincerity. Following are some suggestions that will aid a person to show more enthusiasm vocally:

1. Important words should be emphasized by speaking more slowly. The teacher should stress the words that are important to him for significance.
2. Talking a bit louder will stress the meaning of what is being said. A variation in volume is important in holding the attention of the listeners.
3. The teacher must have variation in the rate at which he speaks. Some things need to be given rapidly while other things need to be given more slowly. Developing variety in tempo also secures attention even if it means pausing. "Employ the dramatic effect of silence," says Hill. "The mind of the person who is listening catches up with the thoughts you have expressed. Hesitation after a word which you wish to emphasize accentuates the emphasis."[26]
4. By speaking with conviction, the teacher's enthusiasm will spread to his students. However, when the subject calls for it, the instructor should keep a smile in his voice, thereby eliminating gruffness even though he may be speaking loudly and rapidly.[27]
5. Lastly, pitch variety is very important. From time to time, the instructor will want to lower the pitch of his voice just for variations, because there is nothing more boring than listening to a lecturer speaking in a monotone. Pitch variety is important in demonstrating enthusiasm with the voice.[28]

Move about the Classroom

Gordon writes that at times a teacher may get in the habit of staying in the same place and in the same position hour after hour and day after day. However, students will get different visual perspectives from the instructor who moves about instead of staying in one spot all day long. And whereas a routine pacing would become as monotonous as standing still, meaningful movement from one side of the room to the other, and occasionally from the back to the front, can add some life to a dead classroom situation.[29]

Show the Value of the Lesson

Eavey says, "Of all the stimuli to learning, perhaps none is more potent than the learner's realization that what he is learning has value."[30] It is the teacher who demonstrates to the pupils the importance of the lesson for their lives. If the teacher does not see any value in the material, how can he enable the students to realize its importance?

Maintain Attention

The enthusiastic teacher works at holding the students' attention. "Gaining and maintaining attention is a prerequisite for effective communications,"[31] writes DeLosier. He believes that by holding the students' attention a teacher can appeal to their interests, concerns, attitudes, opinions, and needs.[32]

A teacher can keep the students' attention by asking questions that not only deal with factual material, but also with matters of interpretation and opinion. By frequently praising the students for their responses, the instructor will create a warm, comfortable atmosphere that produces excitement in the classroom.[33]

Make the Lesson Interesting

An enthusiastic teacher sharpens a student's desire to learn when he makes the lesson interesting. Through his dramatic flair and style, learning comes alive and takes on a new meaning; however, one's teaching performances should vary with grade and developmental levels and with the specific needs of the students.[34]

Some other principles suggested by Klaurens to make the lesson more stimulating follow:

1. The teacher should use examples and illustrations from real life to explain truths and meanings from the lesson.

2. He can also vary the methods of presenting a lesson. Games, drills, contests, demonstrations, lectures, discussions, questions and answers are some of the ways that a teacher may want to differ the presentations.

3. A variety of audio-visuals such as posters, the overhead, the opaque projector, filmstrips, slides, movies, cassette players and record players — all help keep the students interested.

4. The students can help in the use of the above equipment. When the students get involved, they usually get excited about the lesson, and their enthusiasm becomes contagious.[35]

CONCLUSION

Since students respect the teacher who is enthusiastic about his work, the Christian teacher should strive to be excited about teaching. Information without inspiration is ineffective. Teaching that lacks enthusiasm is one of the contributing factors to poor grades; thus as Wilbur writes, "It is the teacher's responsibility to introduce a judicious mixture of inspiration and information when each lesson is presented. The inspiration is the vehicle that carries the information."[36]

FOOTNOTES

[1]I Corinthians 10:31b.

[2]Jeremiah 32:41c.

[3]Dinsdale T. Young, *The Enthusiasm of God* (London: Hodder and Stoughton, Pub., 1905), p. 1.

[4]Isaiah 37:32b.

[5]Young, pp. 3-4.

[6]*Webster's Third New International Dictionary of the English Language*, (1976), s.v. "enthusiasm."

[7]Ibid.

[8]Mr. B. cites MacArthur in "Singing Bee," *The School Musician*, August/September 1968, p. 20.

[9]Barak Rosenshine, "Enthusiastic Teaching: A Research Review," *School Review*, 78 (August 1970), 505.

[10]Ibid.

[11]Ibid., pp. 505-506.

[12]Victor E. Mastin, "Teacher Enthusiasm," *The Journal of Educational Research*, 56 (March 1963), 386.

[13]Charles E. Jones, *Life Is Tremendous* (Wheaton, Illinois: Tyndale House Publishers, 1968), p. 24.

[14]William Phillips Sanford and Willard Hayes Yeager, *Effective Business Speech* (New York: McGraw-Hill Book Company, Inc., 1960), p. 62.

[15]Glenn R. Capp, *How To Communicate Orally* (Engle-Wood Cliffs, N.J.: Prentice-Hall, Inc., 1964), p. 182.

[16]Edward J. Hegarty, *Making What You Say Pay Off* (West Nyack, New York: Parker Publishing Company, Inc., 1968), p. 180.

[17]Mary Lynn Collins, "Effects of Enthusiasm Training on Preservice Elementary Teachers," *Research in Teacher Education*, 19 (January-February 1978), 53.

[18]Mr. B., p. 14.

[19]Ibid.

[20]Kenneth T. Henson, *Secondary Teaching Methods* (Lexington, Massachusetts: D.C. Heath and Company, 1981), p. 81.

[21]Adam M. Drayer, *Problems and Methods in High School Teaching* (Boston: D.C. Heath and Company, 1963), p. 47.

[22]M. Wayne DeLozier, "The Teacher as Performer: The Art of Selling Students on Learning," *Contemporary Education,* 51 (Fall 1979), 19.

[23]Napoleon Hill and W. Clement Stone, *Success Through a Positive Mental Attitude* (Englewood Cliffs, N.J.: Prentice-Hall, Inc., 1972), p. 120.

[24]Rosenshine, p. 508.

[25]Dale Carnegie, *How To Win Friends and Influence People* (New York: Pocket Book, 1974), p. 179.

[26]Hill, p. 122.

[27]Ibid.

[28]Rosenshine, p. 509.

[29]Ted Gordon, "Tricks of the Trade," *The Clearing House,* 22 (January 1948), 288.

[30]C.B. Eavey, *The Art of Effective Teaching* (Grand Rapids, Michigan: Zondervan Publishing House, 1956), p. 135.

[31]DeLosier, p. 21.

[32]Ibid.

[33]Rosenshine, p. 506.

[34]John Van Hoose and Richard E. Hult, Jr., "The Performing Artist Dimension in Effective Teaching," *Contemporary Education,* 51 (Fall 1979), 36.

[35]Mary K. Klaurens, "Work Motivation Psychology and the Learning Process," *Business Education Forum,* 31 (February 1977), p. 26.

[36]Elmer C. Wilbur, "Classroom Awareness: The Control of Influences," *Business Education World,* October 1949, p. 70.

QUESTIONS AND PROBLEMS

1. Why is it difficult to be an enthusiastic teacher all the time?

2. What is your favorite subject to teach? Why is it easier for you to be excited about this subject?

3. Do you remember ever having an enthusiastic teacher? What grade was it? What subject? How did that teacher affect your attitude toward the subject?

4. Is it possible for a teacher to be an enthusiastic teacher and not have a dynamic personality? Explain.

5. It has been said that in order to be an enthusiastic teacher a person must be a bit of a "ham." Would you agree? Why?

6. What would you add to the list of topics under the title "How To Become an Enthusiastic Teacher?"

7. Have you ever known a teacher who was artifical in an attempt to be enthusiastic? What was your reaction to such a teacher?

8. How might an individual become more enthusiastic? What exercises could he practice?

9. Are there some days you do not feel enthusiastic? What do you do to overcome negative feelings and influences? What are some things a teacher should not do when he does not feel enthusiastic?

Attributes Of A Good Teacher

Chapter 10

X
ATTRIBUTES OF A GOOD TEACHER

I do not know that I could make entirely clear to an outsider the pleasure I have in teaching. I had rather earn my living by teaching than any other way. In my mind, teaching is not merely a life work, a profession, an occupation, a struggle; it is a passion. I love to teach.

I love to teach as a painter loves to paint, as a musician loves to play, as a singer loves to sing, as a strong man rejoices to run a race. Teaching is an art — an art so great and so difficult to master that a man or woman can spend a long life at it without realizing much more than his limitations and mistakes, and his distance from the ideal.

But the main aim of my happy days has been to become a good teacher, just as every architect wishes to be a good architect and every professional poet strives toward perfection.

William Lyon Phelps[1]

Who are the "good teachers"? Well, some are men and some are women; they are adults of every age. Some are tall and some are short. Some are physically attractive while others are not. There are those who have a high level of intelligence; still others are very average. Some are vivacious, and others are reserved. Yet they all possess certain traits that set them apart from their colleagues as being good teachers.

It would be sad indeed for a person to say that he never had a good teacher, for most everyone has had at least one person who made a lasting impression on him in the classroom. Such a teacher is one who not only teaches facts but who creates an excitement in the process. Phelps says that excitement in teaching calls for,

... keen imagination, without which no teacher sees beyond the printed page; ... clear-cut purpose, without which a teacher cannot plant a dream in childrens' hearts; ... love and understanding human needs, without which lessons are as sounding brass; ... resourcefulness, without which work becomes dull and routine; ... knowledge-ability, without which teachers fail and flounder; ... technique, without which latent student powers are not aroused; ... enthusiasm, without which no teacher can recall joys of discovery nor pass along those joys of youth.[2]

The mediocrity of some teachers is contagious. Other instructors have little impact upon the lives of their students because they have made teaching a mechanical process. However, the good teacher, according to Baughman, is seldom mediocre, "verve, color, humor, creativity, surprise, and even 'hamming' ... characterize most great teachers."[3] The effective teacher creates impressions that enable pupils to regard a subject in a new and different perspective. With such a teacher the ordinary becomes the unusual, the dull becomes alive, and the dreaded becomes the anticipated.

To the Christian, teaching should take on special significance. Morris says that every call to Christian service is honorable, but the ministry of teaching holds an important place in the Lord's work. Three times in the New Testament the Holy Spirit lists the gifts of the Spirit (Romans 12:4-8; I Corinthians 12:4-11, 27-28; Ephesians 4:7-11), and although all three differ somewhat, in these selections only the gift of prophecy and the gift of teaching are mentioned all three times. The reiteration shows the importance that God places upon these two gifts.[4]

Beautiful buildings, modern equipment, and a developed curriculum are not sufficient for any Christian school because, in actuality, its educational program is only as effective as its teachers. Consequently, there must be an awareness on the part of the administrators regarding the characteristics of successful teachers. It is true that most teachers possess many notable attributes, but effective teachers are set apart by having special traits and qualities that characterize good teachers.[5]

God does not want anyone to be a weak teacher, and He certainly does not desire anyone to be a mediocre teacher. But how can the average instructor improve? He can improve by imitating the good habits of exemplary teachers. Even though the Lord has made everyone different, there are certain qualities good teachers have that should be imitated by others.

What are the characteristics of the good teacher that sets him above his colleagues? What are the traits that other teachers should endeavor to copy? The following qualities are not in any special order, but certainly they would be at the top of anyone's list of what makes a good teacher.

EVERY GOOD TEACHER . . .

Is Sure of His Calling

II Peter 1:10 admonishes every child of God to ". . . give diligence to make your calling . . . sure." If a Christian is not sure of his calling to be a teacher, he will be ". . . unstable in all his ways" (James 1:8b). By realizing that God (through the administration) has placed him in that particular class, the teacher will have confidence that he has been put with those young people to accomplish the work that only he can do.

God desires the teacher to be in charge and to lead. That does not necessitate his being mean or hateful, but it does require being authoritative through the power of the Holy Spirit.

Another admonition to the Christian teacher concerns his walk with God, "I beseech you that ye walk worthy of the vocation wherewith ye are called" (Ephesians 4:1). No Christian teacher will be sure of his calling in the vocation of teaching if he is not walking a godly, separated life for Christ.

Is Demanding . . .

In Academics. Student interest in a subject can be dramatically increased by teachers who place academic demands upon their pupils. Frymier explains, "Today, students want to be challenged more. Most teachers don't realize it, but many students are bored because teachers are not adequately challenging them."[6] Dr. Gordon A. Sabine, vice president for special projects of Michigan State University, made a study in which a sampling of some 1,600 high school students listed their views on teachers. Two characteristics were mentioned most often as typical of a "best" teacher. One of these was "demanding." Students wanted to be made to work hard; they wanted to be stretched. Here are some of the comments from the students:

> My best teacher was the one who made me do the most work.
> She made us work our tails off with papers once a week and daily quizzes, but she taught. She made us understand, which is the great thing about a good teacher.
> He expected more than any other teacher, but when a teacher is good, you don't mind the work.
> She expected stiff stuff and surprisingly, received it from us all.
> He made you work hard enough so that when you got a good grade, you were proud of it.[7]

Miller insists that super teachers are considered to be tough and demanding. They insist that homework be completed on time and then followed-through. They require more reading and outside assignments than others, but never are their requirements just busy work. They usually have evaluation standards that are more rigorous than others.[8] However, when teachers are demanding, students rise to meet their expectations and respect them for it.

In Control. The effective teacher controls the classroom activities to ensure that progress is made in the wide spectrum of learning. In a study done by Emmer and Evertson, it was found that the most productive teachers spent the first week explaining and reminding the young people of procedures and rules, and those rules and procedures were effectively integrated into the whole learning process. If inappropriate behavior occurred, it was stopped promptly.[9] Medley's research found that "effective teachers run more orderly classrooms," in which "their students spent the major part of the school day in structured activities that left little unoccupied time."[10]

Even students felt that discipline and order were necessary in the classroom so that they might not be deprived of the opportunity to learn. Here are a few of the comments from Sabine's study about their worst teachers who could not control their classes:

> He ran such a liberal class that he had no contol over the students. It was not unusual for drug exchanges to take place right in the classroom.
>
> This teacher was wretched. She had no discipline. There was no atmosphere for learning. The lab was blown up four times in one semester.
>
> He let the students rule him. They could cuss him out or just leave the classroom and he didn't try to stop them.
>
> He had no order in the classroom. Everyone would talk and then he would start yelling.[11]

The purpose of positive discipline and consequential control is to create an environment in which students learn not only academics, but also how to live in society with others. When control is not demanded by the teacher, the students are the losers.

Cares about the Students

Holm relates the following story:

> Forty years ago a Johns Hopkins professor gave a group of graduate students this assignment: Go to the slums. Take two hundred boys between the ages of twelve and sixteen, and investigate their background and environment. Then predict their chances for the future.
>
> The students after consulting social statistics, talking to the boys, and compiling as much data as they could, concluded that ninety percent of the boys would spend some time in a penitentiary.
>
> Twenty-five years later another group of graduate students was given the job of testing the predictions. They went back to the slum

area. Some of the "boys" were still there, a few had died, some had moved away, but they got in touch with one hundred eighty of the original two hundred. They found that only four of the group had ever served time.

Why was it that these boys, now men, who lived in a breeding place of crime had such a surprisingly good record? The researchers were continually told: "Well, there was a teacher. . ."

They pressed further and they found that in 75 percent of the cases it was the same woman. The researchers went to this teacher now living in a home for retired teachers. How had she exerted this remarkable influence over a group of slum children? Could she give them any reason why these boys should have remembered her?

No, she said, No, she really couldn't. And, then, thinking back over the years, she said musingly more to herself than to her questioners; "I loved those boys . . ."[12]

It is the capacity to care intensely about something other than one's self that indicates a mature individual, for it is through caring that self-knowledge and self-acceptance develop into self-giving.[13] The giving of one's self as a teacher means helping pupils before school, after school, or whenever. Caring about students may mean giving up a lunch hour to listen to a problem; it may mean helping students on Saturday to raise money for their special project. The teacher who cares is never too busy to listen or to offer a helpful suggestion or to encourage a dejected young person. A recent survey showed that the teacher qualities that secondary school students desire most are concern and time for their students.[14]

Caring also means loving. "Love suffereth long and is kind . . . love beareth all things, believeth all things, hopeth all things, endureth all things. Love never faileth" (I Corinthians 13:4, 7, 8). Sabine reported that the other characteristic of "best" teacher most frequently mentioned by students (the first being "demanding") was that of "caring".

He wasn't the greatest teacher but he did know and care about young people. He also was willing to listen to our problems, school or otherwise, and advise when possible. He cared and that is what counts.

She cared about what happened to you.

He cared. He showed it.

This teacher cared. And no matter how much 'book learning' a person has, it is nothing until he cares.

She was the most lovable and Christian woman I have ever met. She loved her profession and she loved everyone who was a part of it. She showed no prejudices toward any students. Her brilliant and not-so-brilliant students were all very precious to her.[15]

Students know if their teachers truly care for them.

Is Committed to Teaching

Outstanding teachers love teaching in general and like teaching their subject matter in particular. They have a long time ago committed themselves to the career of teaching, and they love their work. They also show their love for their work by their careful preparation for each subject. Not just bound by a textbook, but drawing upon other sources for ideas and stimulation, they work hard to challenge each pupil. Such teachers demonstrate subject matter expertise by answering questions correctly, by using appropriate examples, and by stressing important details of the lesson.[16]

The committed teacher studies extra hours and strives to improve his mind in his teaching areas. Gordon says the "quality of a teacher's mind is important because it is the grinding wheel against which a student sharpens his mind."[17] Being committed means that a teacher will develop a repertoire of teaching skills and all sorts of motivational techniques.[18] He will keep the attention of his class by making the work interesting because of dedication to the task of teaching. Therefore, he will stick to the subject at hand and will not be easily sidetracked by irrelevant questions and comments.

The dedicated instructor makes teaching look easy and does not present it as some laborious task that must be carried out under great stress. On the other hand, the uncommitted teacher declares his misery by making everyone around him unhappy as well. By performing the ordinary in a natural and pleasing manner, the teacher with commitment becomes a pleasure to be around.

Is Cultivating a Good Sense of Humor

Highet says, "One of the most important qualities of a good teacher is humor. Many are the purposes it serves. The most obvious is it keeps the pupils alive and attentive because they never are quite sure what is coming next."[19] Humor can knit the teacher and the pupils together through enjoyment because when people laugh together, they share a pleasant experience. "The power of humor dissipates anxiety, relieves aggression, and reduces stress."[20]

An effective teacher is able to laugh at himself and, thus, show his pupils that he realizes his own inadequacies. By laughing at himself, he helps the young people to mature to a place where they can eventually laugh at themselves. Humorous anecdotes from his own life will sometimes serve as excellent illustrations in teaching a lesson. When the instructor exhibits a sense of humor, he is revealing his philosophy of life. "The possessor of a real sense of humor can take it as well as hand it out, is able to bend without breaking, is poised and relaxed, and takes his duties seriously but not mournfully."[21]

Is Communicating Well with Pupils . . .

Genuine communication on the part of the teacher is one of the greatest sources of stimulation in reaching pupils. Therefore, the teacher is the key that unlocks the potential in each student and that motivates the student to develop for God. The following are specific ways that the good teacher demonstrates to his young people that he has their best interests at heart.

By Being Warm and Friendly. An individual can be friendly and still be in control of the group; however, "students want their teachers to maintain their separateness."[22] A friendly teacher does not have to put himself on the same level as his students by being a buddy or a pal.

Zax believes that making every pupil feel important whether he is slow or bright is another characteristic of the good teacher. He knows that young people are sensitive to the treatment given to all their classmates. He can show affection for the problem and non-problem youngsters alike because he desires to reach everyone in his class.[23]

Radebaugh and Johnson found that "excellent teachers, as a group, tended to possess a style that can be described as conversational in manner, smooth in verbal expression, confident in tone."[24] The conversational manner and confident tone cause the young people to follow their teacher because they believe he knows where he is going.

By Having Positive Expectations. Self-confidence causes the effective teacher to feel sure that they will succeed. One "marked difference between good and bad teachers, according to several studies, is that trait of positive expectations. Good teachers believe their students will succeed — and they do."[25] By expecting the students to learn, they make them learn.

The teacher shows his positive expectations through encouraging students and suggesting improvements. Even helpful criticism can come across as supportive rather than castigating. By his positive comments a teacher gains the students' respect and confidence; they never have a feeling of failure with him.[26]

By Effectively Presenting the Lesson. The successful teacher is one who knows his subject matter thoroughly and is able to demonstrate its importance. The students understand what he says because of his ability to put a lesson on the level of the young people. He presents his lesson effectively through his well chosen examples, the logical progression of his ideas, and his emphasis on important facts.[27] The excellent teacher not only reinforces, summarizes, demonstrates, encourages, and uses visual aids; but he also offers additional explanations, asks students to evaluate, requests meanings, and deliberately attempts to influence the pupils' attitudes.[28]

By Responding to Questions and Comments. The best teachers welcome questions and comments from the students; they do not feel intimidated by students because they know that class participation is healthy to learning. They encourage questions whenever young people do not understand the material; therefore, they never ridicule students for asking questions. Often, the good teacher rephrases the students' questions and comments in order to emphasize key points.

King says by looking directly at the student making a comment or asking a question, the teacher shows his interest and concern. He concentrates on what is being said and asks the young person to clarify or rephrase anything not clear to him, and he also encourages the student to elaborate further when the class is discussing ideas.[30] In short, the above average teacher has developed good listening techniques.

By Attending to the Following. The teacher who communicates with the students endeavors to be fair at all times, and when he makes a mistake, he admits he is wrong. Students appreciate a teacher who declares what is expected of them and holds to it. Young people also respect a teacher who gives them immediate feedback to their questions and comments and who allows them to express their ideas through class discussions. By showing respect for their contributions, the instructor encourages further participation. This type of teacher teaches more than the textbook by presenting supplementary material that creates interest and develops a desire to learn more than the textual material. Such a teacher communicates with his pupils.[31]

Is Enthusiastic

Enthusiasm is one of the labels given to a super teacher. It is demonstrated by dynamic speech mannerisms, gestures, and overall personality. The personality of the teacher must communicate with the age of the young people with whom he works because his attitude will determine to a great extent the outlook the pupils have toward the subject matter. "When the teacher shows enthusiasm and love for books and the wealth of experience they contain, the attitude of the children toward them will be enhanced."[32] The enthusiastic teacher makes the material interesting by getting emotionally involved in his subject; and then, because of his excitement, he gains and holds the attention of the students.

Is Always Learning

Pupils in the super teacher's classroom are inspired to learn, to inquire, and to know because of their teacher's zest for learning. He arouses their desires to broaden their understanding. He excites their curiosity and creates new interests that they never had before. Because he is always learning, he is able to share his knowledge with the young people and thus to become the leader of their interests. Eavey says that a continuous desire to challenge his pupils motivates him to become a better teacher.[33] And, Eavey continues,

> An effective teacher never becomes a finished product. His reach forever exceeds his grasp. Always, there are horizons beyond which lies new territory to be explored, new ideas to replenish the mind, new challenges to develop skill to higher levels, new problems to be mastered, further study to be done, and ever-present need for finding better ways to apply the principles and laws of learning and teaching in every day practice.[34]

Is Loyal

"A lack of loyalty to leadership will destroy an organization. As the group must be loyal to the leader, he in turn must be loyal to them."[35] Thus, says Engstrom, the strong teacher demonstrates loyalty through his devotion and faithfulness to his students. His confidence in his students' worth and capabilities is reciprocated through their loyalty to him. Pupils desire to follow an individual who has their interests at heart; and to such a person, young people will give cooperation, obedience and loyal support.[36]

Loyalty to the church, to the pastor, to the principal, to the whole school organization are all characteristics of a great Christian teacher. If an individual is not loyal in these areas, he will be unhappy and dissatisfied, and his lack of loyalty will produce rebellious and discontented followers. Loyalty is the oil that enables the operations of a school to run smoothly.

Sets Goals

Mills writes that the excellent teacher sets goals for his talents, his interests, his knowledge, his personality, and his self-potentiality. He strives to have the qualities of a good teacher: helpfulness, kindness, cheerfulness, consideration, appreciation, industry, tact, patience, fairness, courtesy, sympathy, cooperation, discretion, honesty, impartiality, promptness, modesty, morality, and courage.[37]

The Christian teacher who excels sets spiritual goals for his life. He realizes that he has a tremendous responsibility every day to examine himself, his convictions, and his motives. Outwardly he must fulfill the work that the Lord desires of him by being "filled with the Spirit" (Ephesians 5:18) and by being "an example of the believers" (I Timothy 4:12-13).[38] In addition to his outward responsibility, he must endeavor to know the Scriptures better and better that he might integrate its truths into his subject matter every day.

CONCLUSION

The good teacher has the characteristics mentioned in this chapter. He is aware that he has failed when he makes teaching look hard and tedious or when he makes learning appear to be something that is distasteful. The good teacher, however, presents his material in such a way that his pupils not only work hard but also enjoy it. And because of all these things, his students know him to be a great teacher. Koerin continues,

> The effective teacher is one whose presentation of the subject matter is interesting, skillful and organized; who exhibits skill in controlling and facilitating group interaction; and who is responsive, accessible and interested in the individual student as a person. Additionally, the effective teacher is enthusiastic about the subject matter and about teaching itself.[39]

There is no magical process, no set method, no perfect formula for being a good teacher; but there is plenty of hard work and a great deal of effort. However, when the Christian teacher earnestly endeavors to be a good teacher for the glory of the Lord Jesus Christ, God will enable him to achieve his goals, for the Lord desires that every teaching servant of His be a great teacher.

FOOTNOTES

[1]Edwin John Brown, *Managing the Classroom* (New York: The Roland Press Company, 1952), p. 413.

[2]William Lyon Phelps, *Autobiography* cited in "Which Students Are Yours?", *Today's Education*, 62 (March 1973), 20-21.

[3]M. Dale Baughman, "Teaching with Humor: A Performing Art," *Contemporary Education*, 51 (Fall 1979), 27.

[4]Henry M. Morris, *Education for the Real World* (San Diego, Calif.: Creation Life Publishers, 1977), p. 153.

[5]Hubert H. Mills and Harl R. Douglas, *Teaching in High School* (New York: The Ronald Press Co., 1957), p. 32.

[6]Jack Frymier, "Address to Southwest Educational Research Association," as cited in *Secondary Teaching Methods* (Lexington, Massachusetts: D.C. Heath and Company, 1981), p. 83.

[7]Gordon A. Sabine, *How Students Rate Their Schools and Teachers* (Washington, D.C.: Published by National Association of Secondary School Principals, 1971), pp. 6-7.

[8]Mary Sue Miller, "What Makes Superteachers Super?" *Instructor*, Fall 1980, p. 16.

[9]Edmund T. Emmer and Carolyn M. Everston, "Effective Classroom Management at the Beginning of the School Year," *The Elementary School Journal*, 80 (May 1980), 225.

[10]Ullik Rouk quoting Medley in "What Makes an Effective Teacher?" *American Educator*, 32 (Fall 1980), 16.

[11]Sabine, p. 20.

[12]James N. Holm, *Tested Methods of Teaching Speech* (Portland, Maine: Weston Walch, Publisher, 1962), pp. 21-22.

[13]Harry and Bonaro Overstreet, *The Mind Alive* cited by Evelyn Wenzel, *Creativity in Teaching* (Belmont, California: Wadsworth Publishing Co., Inc., 1961), p. 50.

[14]Kenneth T. Henson, *Secondary Teaching: A Personal Approach* (Itasca, Ill.: F.E. Peacock, 1974), pp. 3-4.

[15]Sabine, pp. 24-25.

[16]Pete Potamianos and Lynn Crilly, "Grade 'A' Instructor: How Do You Know One When You See One?," *NSPI Journal,* 19 (June 1980), 24.

[17]Edward J. Gordon, "The Effective English Teacher," *English Journal,* 62 (March 1973), 448.

[18]"Classified — for Administrators Only," *Instructor,* (January 1981), p. 24.

[19]Gilbert Highet, *The Art of Teaching* as cited in "Teaching with Humor: A Performing Art," *Contemporary Education,* 51 (Fall 1979), 28.

[20]Baughman, p. 30.

[21]Ibid.

[22]Sabine, p. 33.

[23]Manuel Zax, "Outstanding Teachers: Who Are They?" *The Clearing House,* 45 (January 1971), 288.

[24]Byron F. Radebaugh and James A. Johnson, "Phase II Excellent Teachers: What Makes Them Outstanding?" *The Clearing House,* 45 (March 1971), 413.

[25]"Classified . . .," p. 63.

[26]Richard P. Manatt, Kenneth L. Palmer, and Everett Hildebaugh, "Evaluating Teacher Performance with Improved Rating Scales," *NASSP Bulletin,* 60 (September 1976), 22.

[27]Betty S. Johnson, "Communication: Key to Effective Teaching," *Journal for Business Education,* 55 (March 1980), 264.

[28]Radebaugh, p. 412.

[29]Potamianos, p. 25.

[30]Richard A. King, "Reliable Rating Sheets: A Key to Effective Teacher Evaluation," *NASSP Bulletin,* 62 (December 1978), 22-23.

[31]"Classified . . .," p. 65.

[32]Oscar T. Jarvis and Lutian R. Wootton, *The Transitional Elementary School and Its Curriculum* (Dubuque, Iowa: Wm. C. Brown Company Publishers, 1966), p. 184.

[33]C.B. Eavey, *The Art of Effective Teaching* (Grand Rapids, Michigan: Zondervan Publishing House, 1953), pp. 33-34.

[34]Ibid., p. 34.

[35]Ted W. Engstrom, *The Making of a Christian Leader* (Grand Rapids, Michigan: Zondervan Publishing House, 1976), p. 89.

[36]James K. Van Fleet, *The 22 Biggest Mistakes Managers Make and How to Correct Them* (West Nyack, N.Y.: Parker Publishing Company, Inc., 1973), p. 39

[37]Mills, p. 33.

[38]Morris, pp. 152-153.

[39]Beverly B. Koerin, "Teaching Effectiveness and Faculty Development Programs: A Review," *JGE: The Journal of General Education,* 32 (Spring 1980), 45.

QUESTIONS AND PROBLEMS

1. How many unusually effective teachers have you had in school? Did you realize at the time that they were above average? Why?

2. What other characteristics of a good teacher can you think of that are not mentioned in this chapter?

3. What do you consider to be the most important characteristic of a good teacher? Why did you pick this?

4. How could good teachers be used more effectively in their schools?

5. Do you think that some administrators are intimidated by good teachers? What should an administrator's attitude be toward a good teacher?

6. Is it possible for every teacher to be a good teacher? Do you think God is pleased with a teacher being average? Explain

7. Which of the characteristics mentioned in this chapter do you consider to be your strongest? Your weakest?

8. What are you doing **now** to develop as a better teacher? What do you plan to do in the future to develop more characteristics of a good teacher?

BIBLIOGRAPHY

Alexander, William M. and Halverson, Paul M. *Effective Teaching in Secondary Schools.* New York: Rinehart and Company, 1956.

Allen, Charles. *God's Psychiatry.* Westwood: Fleming H. Revell Co., 1953.

Axelrod, Sal; Hall, R. Hal; and Tams, Ann. "Comparison of Two Common Classroom Seating Arrangements," *Academic Therapy* 15 (September 1979): 35.

Bagley, William Chandler. *Classroom Management.* New York: The Macmillan Company, 1911.

Baker, A.A. *The Successful Christian School.* Pensacola, Florida: A Beka Book Publications, 1979.

Baughman, M. Dale. "Teaching With Humor: A Performing Art." *Contemporary Education* 51 (Fall 1979): 27.

Benson, Clarence H. *The Sunday School in Action.* Chicago: Moody Press, 1953.

Berry, Ray. *Practical Child Training.* Pleasant Hill, Ohio: The Parents Association Publishers, n.d.

Betts, G.H. *The Teaching of Religion* quoted in *A Christian Pedagogy.* New Ulm, Minnesota: Martin Albrecht Publisher, n.d.

Blaney, Robert L. "Effective Teaching in Early Childhood Education." *The Elementary School Journal.* 80 (January 1980): 128.

Bossing, Nelson L. *Teaching in Secondary Schools.* 3rd ed. Boston: Houghton Mifflin Company, 1952.

Bradley, Barbara. "Elementary Discipline." *Philosophy of Discipline Syllabus.* Pensacola, Florida: A Beka Book Publications.

Brophy, Jere E. "Advances in Teacher Research." *The Journal of Classroom Interaction.* 15 (Winter 1979): 3.

Brown, Edwin John. *Managing the Classroom.* New York: The Roland Press Company, 1952.

Brown, Edwin John and Phelps, Arthur Thomas. *Managing the Classroom.* 2nd ed. New York: The Ronald Press Company, 1961.

Buffington, Perry W. "Of Tests and Techniques," *Sky* May 1981, p. 32.

Byrne, H.W. *A Christian Approach to Education.* Milford, Mich.: Mott Media, 1971.

Byrne, H.W. *Christian Education for the Local Church.* Grand Rapids, Michigan: Zondervan Publishing House, 1973.

Callahan, Sterling G. *Successful Teaching in Secondary Schools.* Glenview, Illinois: Scott, Foresman and Company, 1971.

Campbell, Doak S. *When Do Teachers Teach?* Nashville, Tennessee: Broadman Press, 1935.

Capp, Glenn R. *How to Communicate Orally.* Englewood Cliffs, N.J.: Prentice-Hall, Inc., 1964.

Carnegie, Dale. *How To Win Friends and Influence People.* New York: Pocket Book, Publishers, 1974.

Carter, William L.; Hansen, Carl W.; and McKim, Margaret S. *Learning to Teach in the Secondary School.* New York: The MacMillan Company, 1962.

Chalmers, Thomas cited in *Gems from Christian Writers.* London: W. Clowes and Sons, n.d.

Chapman, Marie M. *Practical Methods for Sunday School Teachers.* Grand Rapids, Michigan: Zondervan Publishing House, 1962.

Christiansen, Ted. "10 Commandments of Classroom Discipline." *New Mexico School Review* Vol. 48.

"Classified — for Administrators Only." *Instructor* 90 (January 1981): 63.

Collins, Mary Lynn. "Effects of Enthusiasm Training on Preservice Elementary Teachers." *Research in Teacher Education.* January-February 1978.

Collins, Myrtle and Collins, Dwane R. *Survival Kit for Teachers (and Parents).* Pacific Palesades, Calif.: The Goodyear Publishing Co., 1975.

Crow, Lester D. and Crow, Alice. *The Student Teacher in the Elementary School.* New York: David McKay Co., Inc., 1965.

Deane, Anthony C. *Jesus Christ.* London: Hodder and Stoughton, 1935.

DeLozier, M. Wayne. "The Teacher as Performer: The Art of Selling Students on Learning." *Contemporary Education.* 51 (Fall 1979): 19.

DeZafra, Jr., Carlos. *62 Suggestions to Improve Classroom Discipline.* Fairfield, New Jersey: The Economic Press, Inc., 1968.

Doan, Eleanor L. *The Speaker's Sourcebook.* Grand Rapids: Zondervan Publishing House, 1971.

Dobson, James. *Dare to Discipline.* Wheaton, Ill.: Tyndale House Pub., 1973.

Dobson, James. *Hide or Seek.* Old Tappan, N.J.: Fleming H. Revell Co., 1974.

Drayer, Adam M. *Problems and Methods in High School Teaching.* Boston: D.C. Heath and Company, 1963.

Eavey, C.B. "Aims and Objectives of Christian Education." *An Introduction to Evangelical Christian Education* edited by J. Edward Hakes. Chicago: Moody Press, 1964.

Eavey, C.B. *Principles of Teaching for Christian Teachers.* Grand Rapids, Michigan: Zondervan Publishing House, 1971.

Eavey, C.B. *The Art of Effective Teaching.* Grand Rapids, Michigan: Zondervan Publishing House, 1956.

Eble, Kenneth E. *The Craft of Teaching.* Washington: Jossey-Bass Publishers, 1976.

Edmunds, Emma and White, Gayle. "Principal Is Key To Orderly School." *The Atlanta Constitution.* 9 June 1978 sec. B, p. 1.

Emmer, Edmund T., and Evertson, Carolyn M. "Effective Classroom Management at the Beginning of the School Year." *The Elementary School Journal* 80 (May 1980): 225.

Engstrom, Ted W. *The Making of a Christian Leader.* Grand Rapids, Michigan: Zondervan Publishing House, 1976.

Fine, Benjamine, and Fine, Lillian. *How to Get the Best Education for Your Child.* New York: G.P. Putman's Sons, 1959.

Fine, Benjamine. *Your Child and School.* New York: The Macmillan Company, 1965.

Fremont, Walter G. "Building Character in Youth," *Balance.* Greenville, South Carolina: Bob Jones University Press.

Fremont, Walter G. "Christian Character Development," *Voice of the Alumni.* Greenville, South Carolina: Bob Jones University Press, April 1973.

Frymier, Jack. Address to Southwest Educational Research Association. Second Annual Meeting. quoted in Kenneth T. Henson, *Secondary Teaching Metthods.* Lexington, Massachusetts: D.C. Heath and Company, 1981.

Fuller, Andrew cited in *Gems from Christian Writers.* London: W. Clowes and Sons, n.d.

Gaebelein, Frank E. *The Pattern of God's Truth.* Chicago: Moody Press, 1968.

Gangel, Kenneth O. *Leadership for Church Education.* Chicago: Moody Press, 1970.

Gangel, Kenneth O., *Understanding Teaching.* Wheaton, Illinois: Evangelical Teacher Training Association, 1968.

Garwood, S. Gray. "Ten Ways to Prevent Classroom Chaos," *Instructor* 94 (October 1976): 75.

Gettys, Joseph M. *How to Teach Bible.* Richmond, Virginia: John Knox Press, 1966.

Good, Thomas and Brophy, Jere. *Looking in Classrooms.* New York: Harper and Row publ., 1973.

Goodman, George. *What To Teach and How To Reach the Young.* London: Pickering and Inglis Ltd., 1946.

Gordon, Edward J. "The Effective English Teacher." *English Journal* 62 (March 1973): 448.

Gordon, Ted. "Tricks of the Trade." *The Clearing House.* 22 (January 1948): 288.

Gray, Jenny. *The Teacher's Survival Guide.* Palo Alto, California: Fearon Publishers, 1967.

Gronlund, Norman E. *Measurement and Evaluation in Teaching* 4th ed. New York: MacMillan Publishing Co., Inc., 1981.

Gruhn, William T. and Douglas, Harl R. *The Modern Junior High School.*

New York: The Ronald Press Company, 1947.

Hakes, J. Edward. *An Introduction to Evangelical Christian Education.* Chicago: Moody Press, 1964.

Hegarty, Edward J. *Making What You Say Pay Off.* West Nyack, New York: Parker Publishing Company, Inc. 1968.

Hein, Lucille. *Enjoy Your Children.* New York: Abingdon Press, 1959.

Henson, Kenneth T. *Secondary Teaching: A Personal Approach.* Itasca, Ill.: F.E. Peacock, 1974.

Henson, Kenneth T. *Secondary Teaching Methods.* Lexington, Massachusetts: D.C. Heath and Company, 1981.

Hicks, Laurel. "Character Training vs. Behavior Modification," as quoted in A.A. Baker, *The Successful Christian School.* Pensacola, Florida: A Beka Book Publications, 1979.

Highet, Gilbert. *The Art of Teaching.* New York: Alfred A. Knopf Pub., 1973.

Highet, Gilbert. *The Art of Teaching.* cited by Dale M. Baughman. "Teaching With Humor: A Performing Art." *Contemporary Education* 51 (Fall 1979): 28.

Hill, Napoleon and Stone, W. Clement. *Success Through a Positive Mental Attitude.* Englewood Cliffs, N.J.: Prentice-Hall, Inc., 1971.

Holm, James N. *Tested Methods of Teaching Speech.* Portland, Maine: J. Weston Walch, Publisher, 1962.

Hoover, Kenneth H. *Learning and Teaching in the Secondary School.* Boston: Allyn and Bacon, Inc., 1965.

Howse, W.L. *Those Treasured Hours.* Nashville, Tennessee: Broadman Press, 1960.

Hughes, H. Treavor. *Faith and Life.* London: Cox and Wyman, Ltd., 1962.

Hyles, Jack. *Blue Denim and Lace.* Hammond, Indiana: Hyles-Anderson Publishers, 1969.

Hyles, Jack. *Grace and Truth.* Hammond, Indiana: Hyles-Anderson Pub., 1975.

Hyles, Jack, Sermon on "Character" as printed in *Rebirth of Our Nation.* Accelerated Christian Education, 1979.

Inlow, Gail M. *Maturity in High School.* Englewood Cliffs, New Jersey: Prentice-Hall, Inc., 1963.

Inlow, Gail M. *Maturity in The High School Teaching.* Englewood Cliffs, New Jersey: Prentice-Hall, Inc., 1963.

Institute in Basic Youth Conflicts Syllabus. Oak Brook, Ill.

Jarvis, Oscar T., and Wootton, Lutian R. *The Transitional Elementary School and Its Curriculum.* Dubuque, Iowa: Wm. C. Brown Company Publishers, 1966.

Johnson, Betty S. "Communication: Key to Effective Teaching." *Journal for Business Education* 55 (March 1980): 264.

Johnson, Thelma. "Kindergarten Discipline and Habits." *Philosophy of Discipline Syllabus.* Pensacola, Florida: A Beka Book Publications.

Jones, Bob, Jr. "Editorial," *Faith for the Family.* February 1981.

Jones, Charles E. *Life Is Tremendous.* Wheaton, Illinois: Tyndale House Publishers, 1968.

Jones, Frederic H. "The Gentle Art of Classroom Discipline." *Elementary School Principals Journal.* July 1979.

Karlin, Muriel Schoenbrun and Berger, Regina. *Discipline and the Disruptive Child.* West Nyack, NY: Parker Pub., Co., Inc., 1972.

Kindsuatter, Richard. "A New View of the Dynamics of Discipline." *Phi Delta Kappan.* January 1978.

King, Richard A. "Reliable Rating Sheets: A Key to Effective Teacher Evaluation." *NASSP Bulletin* 62 (December 1978): 22-23.

Klaurens, Mary K. "Work Motivation Psychology and the Learning Process." *Business Education Forum.* 31 (February 1977): 26.

Koehler, Edward A. *A Christian Pedagogy.* New Ulm, Minn.: Martin Albrecht Publisher, 1930.

Koerin, Beverly B. "Teaching Effectiveness and Faculty Development Programs: A Review." *JGE: The Journal of General Education* 32 (Spring 1980): 45.

LaHaye, Beverly. *How To Develop Your Child's Temperament.* Irvine: Harvest House Pub., 1977.

Langdon, Grace and Stout, Irving W. *Homework.* New York: The John Day Company, 1969.

Leavitt, Guy P. *Teach With Success.* Cincinnati, Ohio: Standard Publishing, 1956.

Lien, Arnold J. *Measurement and Evaluation of Learning.* 3rd ed. Dubuque, Iowa: Wm. C. Brown Company Publishers, 1976.

Mr. B. cites *MacArthur* in "Singing Bee." *The School Musician.* August-September, 1968, p. 20.

Malone, Tom. *Essentials of Evangelism.* Murfreesboro, Tennessee: Sword of the Lord Publishers, 1958.

Manatt, Richard P.; Palmer, Kenneth L.; and Hildebaugh, Everett. "Evaluating Teacher Performance with Improved Rating Scales." *NASSP Bulletin* 60 (September 1976): 22.

Marshall, John Clark and Hales, Loyde Wessley. *Essentials of Testing.* Reading, Massachusetts: Addison-Wesley Publishing Company, 1972.

Mastin, Victor E. "Teacher Enthusiasm." *The Journal of Educational Research.* 56 (March 1963): 386.

May, Philip. *Which Way to Educate?* Chicago: Moody Press. 1975.

McDonald, Blanch and Nelson, Leslie. *Successful Classroom Control.* Dubuque, Iowa: Wm. C. Brown Co., 1955.

McKnown, Harry C. *Character Education.* New York: McGraw-Hill Book Company, Inc., 1935.

McPhie, Walter E. "Discipline Problems: An Educational Malignancy." *National Association of Secondary School Principals.* December 1961.

Mehl, Marie A; Mills, Hubert H.; and Douglas, Harl R. *Teaching in Elementary School.* New York: The Ronald Press Company, 1958.

Miller, J.R. *The Building of Character.* London: The Sunday School Union, n.d.

Miller, Mary Sue. "What Makes Superteachers Super?" *Instructor* 87 (October 1977): 120.

Mills, Herbert and Douglas, Harl R. *Teaching in High School.* 2nd. ed. New York: The Ronald Press Company, 1957.

Mills, Herbert H., and Douglas, Harl R. *Teaching in High School.* New York: The Roland Press Co., 1957.

Morris, Henry M. *Education for the Real World.* San Diego, Calif.: Creation Life Publishers, 1977 .

Morse, William C. and Wingo, G. Max. *Psychology and Teaching.* 3rd ed. Atlanta: Scott, Foresman Co., 1969.

Murray, Andrew. *The School of Obedience.* London: Marshall, Morgan, and Scott Ltd., n.d.

Mursell, James L. *The Psychology of Secondary School.* New York: W.W. Norton and Company, Inc., 1932.

Overstreet, Harry and Bonaro. *The Mind Alive.* cited by Evelyn Wenzel. *Creativity in Teaching.* Belmont, California: Wadsworth Publishing Co., Inc., 1961.

Page, Ellis B. "Teacher Comments and Student Performance: A Seventy-four Classroom Experiment in School Motivation," *Journal of Educational Psychology.* 48 (August 1958): pp. 173-181.

Parker, Percy G. *The Model Christian.* London: Victory Press, 1933.

Pennell, William W. *Church Leadership Seminar.* Decatur, Georgia: Forrest Hills Baptist Church, n.d.

Pennell, William W., "Faith." Sunday School Lesson, Forrest Hills Baptist Church, Decatur, Georgia. (Mimeograph)

Phelps, William Lyon. *Autobiography.* quoted by Michael J. Sexton "Which Students Are Yours?" *Today's Education* 62 (March 1973): 20-21.

Potamianos, Pete, and Crilly, Lynn. "Grade 'A' Instructor: How Do You Know One When You See One?" *NSPI Journal* 19 (June 1980): 24.

Radebaugh, Bryon F., and Johnson, James A. "Phase II Excellent Teachers: What Makes Them Outstanding?" *The Clearing House* 45 (March 1971): 413.

Rafferty, Max. *Max Rafferty on Education.* New York: The Devin-Adair Company, 1968.

Redpath, Alan. *Learning to Live*. Grand Rapids, Mich.: Wm. B. Erdman's Pub. Co., 1962.

Rickover, H.G. *Education and Freedom*. New York: E.P. Dutton and Company, Inc., 1959.

Robinson, Francis P. *Effective Study*. New York: Harper and Row, Publishers, 1961.

Rosenshine, Barak. "Enthusiastic Teaching: A Research Review." *School Review*. 78 (August 1970): 505.

Rouk, Ullik. "What Makes an Effective Teacher?" *American Educator* 32 (Fall 1980): 16.

Rozell, Ray. *Talks on Sunday School Teaching*. Grand Rapids, Michigan: Zondervan Publishing House, 1969.

Rudman, Marsha. "Discipline." *Instructor*. August/September 1976.

Sabine, Gordon A. *How Students Rate Their Schools and Teachers*. Washington, D.C.: Published by National Association of Secondary School Principals, 1971.

Samalonis, Bernice L. *Methods and Materials for Today's High School*. New York: Van Nostrand Reinhold Company, 1970.

Sanford, William Phillips and Yeager, Willard Hayes. *Effective Business Speech*. New York: McGraw-Hill Book Company, Inc., 1960.

Schaefer, Charles E. "Practice Exchange on Punishment." *Child Quarterly*. 5 (Winter 1976): 308.

Schaffer, Ronald. *Temple Heights Christian School Handbook*. A Ministry of Temple Heights Baptist Church. Tampa, Florida, 1978.

Schain, Robert L. and Polner, Murray. *Using Effective Discipline for Better Class Control*. New York: Teachers Practical Press, Inc., 1966.

Schwartz, Alfred and Tiedeman, S.C. *Evaluating Student Progress in the Secondary School*. New York: Longman, Green and Co., David McKay Co., 1957.

Shaheen, JoAnn. "Guidelines for Discipline." quoted by Eugene R. Howard, *School Discipline Desk Book*. West Nyack, N.Y.: Parker Pub. Co., Inc., 1978.

Sholund, Milford. "Teaching Junior High School Youth," *An Introduction to Evangelical Christian Education*. edited by J. Edward Hakes. Chicago: Moody Press, 1972.

Silberman, Charles E. *Crisis in the Classroom*. New York: Random House, 1970.

Simpson, A.B. *Standing on Faith*. London: Marshall, Morgan and Scott Ltd., 1934.

Smiles, Samuel. *Character*. New York: A.L. Burt, Publisher, n.d.

Smith, Thomas. "The Christian Philosophy of Discipline." *The Christian Educator*. Vol. 2 January 1976.

Smith, Thomas. *What Every Parent Should Know about Christian Education.* Murfreesboro, Tenn.: Christian Educator Publications, 1976.

Sorenson, Herbert. *Psychology in Education.* New York: McGraw-Hill Book Co., 1964.

Stanfield, V.L. *The Christian Worshipping.* Nashville: Convention Press, 1965.

Stevens, Andrew. "Techniques for Handling Problem Parents." *Handbook of Successful School Administration.* Englewood Cliffs, New Jersey: Prentice-Hall, Inc., 1976.

Stoddard, George D. *The Out-Look for American Education.* Carbondale, Illinois: Southern Illinois University Press, 1974.

Teacher's Handbook. Pensacola Christian School, A Beka Book Publications, Pensacola, Florida.

Tiedt, Sidney W. and Tiedt, Iris M. *The Elementary Teacher's Complete Handbook.* Englewood Cliffs, New Jersey: Prentice-Hall, Inc., 1965.

Torrey, R.A. *Personal Work.* Westwood, N.J.: Fleming H. Revell Company, n.d.

Trumbull, H. Clay. *Teaching and Teachers.* New York: Charles Scribner's Sons, 1906.

Tyler, Ralph W. "The Problems and Possibilities of Educational Evolution," *The Schools and the Challenge of Innovation.* New York: McGraw-Hill Book Company, 1969.

Van Fleet, James K. *The 22 Biggest Mistakes Managers Make and How to Correct Them.* West Nyack, N.Y.: Parker Publishing Company, Inc., 1973.

Van Hoose, John and Hult, Richard E. Jr., "The Performing Artist Dimension in Effective Teaching." *Contemporary Education.* 51 (Fall 1979): 36.

Vogelheim, R.M. "Effect of Social Reinforcement on Poor Posture," cited in *Therapies for School Behavior Problems.* San Francisco: Jossey-Bass Publishers. 1980.

Walton, John. *Toward Better Teaching in the Secondary Schools.* Boston: Allyn and Bacon, 1966.

Weaver, Galen R. "The Teacher Being An Example of Self-Discipline," *Chronicle of Christian Education.* Bangor, Maine: Maine Association of Christian Schools, October 1981.

Webster's Third New International Dictionary (Unabridged) Springfield, Mass: G. & C. Merriam Company, Publishers, 1963.

Webster's Third New International Dictionary of the English Language. unabridged, 1976 ed. S. v. "Enthusiasm."

Whalen, Thomas J. "Homework," compiled by James A. Johnson and Roger C. Anderson. *Secondary Student Teaching Readings.* Glenview, Illinois: Scott, Foresman and Company, 1971.

Wilbur, Elmer C. "Classroom Awareness: The Control of Influence." *Business Education World*. October 1949, p. 70.

Wilkes, L. *Teach Yourself to Teach*. London: English Universities Press, Ltd., 1953.

Wilson, Clifford A. *Jesus the Teacher*. Melbourne, Australia: Word of Truth Productions Ltd., 1974.

Wood, G.R. Harding. *Learning and Living the Christian Life*. Roanoke, Va.: Progress Press, 1976.

Young, Dinsdale T. *The Enthusiasm of God*. London: Hodder and Stoughton, Pub., 1905.

Zax, Manuel. "Outstanding Teachers: Who Are They?" *The Clearing House* 45 (January 1971): 288.

Because of the scarcity of subject matter regarding Christian education, the author has had to use some sources which he cannot wholly endorse in the areas of philosophy or theology.